I'm delighted to see Georgia's expertise in delivering constructive feedback now being widely recognised. Early in my career, and when I then reported to Georgia, I experienced her talent in this area, firsthand. Delivering effective feedback is a misunderstood and often downplayed art; and one which we can all grow better at.

— **Matthew Chapman**, CEO, ChapmanCG

Everything you need to fix feedback is brought together into one powerful package. *Fixing Feedback* is a common sense, plain English guidebook to that most important of interactions — the feedback conversation. Georgia Murch shows us why they are important, the evidence about what works, how to approach them and how to find your flow to a high-performance workplace.

— **Paul Duldig**, Head of University Services,
The University of Melbourne

The journey to remarkable is a revolving dance of three steps forward and two steps back. In robust style, Georgia shows how to construct and enjoy the forward steps and learn from the back steps — and perhaps sidestep them in the future. Georgia provides a wealth of contemporary thinking, accompanied by many personal and professional examples. Read, reflect and try the journey to remarkable.

— **Tim Orton**, Managing Director, The Nous Group

FIXING
FEEDBACK

FIXING
FEEDBACK

GEORGIA MURCH

WILEY

First published in 2016 by John Wiley & Sons Australia, Ltd
42 McDougall St, Milton Qld 4064
Office also in Melbourne

Typeset in 11/13 pt Palatino LT Std Light by Aptara, India

National Library of Australia Cataloguing-in-Publication data:

Creator:	Murch, Georgia, author.
Title:	Fixing Feedback / Georgia Murch.
ISBN:	9780730327462 (pbk.)
	9780730329718 (custom)
	9780730327479 (ebook)
Notes:	Includes index.
Subjects:	Feedback (Psychology)
	Interpersonal communication.
	Communication in personnel management.
	Communication in organizations.
Dewey Number:	153.6

Cover design by Wiley

Cover image © Epifantsev/iStockphoto

Printed in Singapore by C.O.S. Printers Pte Ltd

10 9 8 7 6 5 4 3 2 1

Disclaimer
The material in this publication is of the nature of general comment only, and does not represent professional advice. It is not intended to provide specific guidance for particular circumstances and it should not be relied on as the basis for any decision to take action or not take action on any matter which it covers. Readers should obtain professional advice where appropriate, before making any such decision. To the maximum extent permitted by law, the author and publisher disclaim all responsibility and liability to any person, arising directly or indirectly from any person taking or not taking action based on the information in this publication.

CONTENTS

ABOUT THE AUTHOR

Georgia is obsessed with the power of great communication. She knows how great communication leads to great collaboration and helps create outstanding cultures. She sees the profound impact communication has on the success of businesses. Remarkable conversations make businesses better.

Georgia understands the importance of delivering programs that impact the bottom line. By helping people have constructive conversations, and giving leaders the confidence to lead with ease, Georgia helps businesses become highly productive by leveraging the power of their people.

She's an expert in helping others master the art of conversation. By creating a culture based on trust and respect, she helps create environments that let clever people get on with being clever, so companies can navigate change smoothly, hold on to their brightest sparks and let their leaders spend their time on the things that matter.

Georgia has over 20 years of experience working with public and private organisations of all shapes and sizes, in Australia and overseas. She has worked in consulting, designing and facilitating leadership, cultural change and customer-focused programs. This deep experience means she truly appreciates the diversity and challenge of complex workforces and understands the complexity of managing a business while leading change.

She now works with savvy, fast-paced organisations and leaders to help create remarkable communicators — so remarkable that people can't stop talking about them and things just get done.

Visit georgiamurch.com to find out more about Georgia, what she does and what she's been thinking about lately. You can also find her on Facebook and Twitter (@GeorgiaMurch), and connect with her on LinkedIn.

ACKNOWLEDGEMENTS

Writing this has cemented how passionate I am about what I know. It has held me to account to be the person I challenge others to be.

Matt Church and Pete Cook—you made me do it! Thank god you did. Thank you to those leaders and mentors who lead from the space that I admire and have helped shape who I am today. Paul Jury and Tim Orton are two of the most authentic leaders I have had the privilege of working for. Geoff Morgan stayed close and reminded me that the human side of leadership wins over strategy every time. Thank you to mentors and friends like Gabrielle Dolan and Annie Layton, who challenge me in a way that inspires rather than tells. Great women who are authentic and walk the talk.

It's not just the obvious people I'm grateful for. Those who don't demand attention through their title or position have taught me just as much. Thank you to the grumpy guy at the drycleaner it took me six years to get a smile from; to the lady at the local coffee shop who always asked how I was, and meant it. Special mention to John Douglas and Caroline Thurling for your professional wisdom and personal support. I will always be grateful.

Thank you to my clients, many of whom I am now lucky to call friends. It's been such a great ride. I am blessed to do work I love with people I value and enjoy, and I don't take it for granted.

High-five and much gratitude to Lucy Raymond from Wiley, for believing in this book and helping me to get the message out there.

And to my friends and family, who have remained gracious and patient while I continue to work on my style, my 'rightness' and my need to verbally process. Your elegance of friendship, your casual reminders and your commitment to the end makes me so proud. I am proud to be in the trenches of life with you.

Jackson and Holly, two of my best teachers, through the joy and hard work of parenting. You are two of the most impressive humans I know. Your love, laughter and thirst for life will forever impress and inspire me.

And then there's my dear old Dad. I have learnt so much from you. Many of these lessons and observations have shaped the person who I am. I hope you receive as much from this as I have been blessed to receive. I know Mum would be so proud, too.

INTRODUCTION

After more than 20 years working, leading, managing and consulting, it's clear to me that the number one thing that gets in the way of people being awesome is ... being a dick!

Do I really need to explain what 'being a dick' means? I did some research, and apparently 'being a dick' is a common phenomenon. It knows no bounds. It spans nationalities, cultures, industries and disciplines. When I mention the subtitle of this book, the near first thing that people say is, 'I could buy that book for someone I work with'.

We all know people who are not cool to work with. These people often say the wrong thing, lack self-awareness, let their ego walk in the door before they do, and have a natural talent for being a dick. But if we dare to be truly honest, most of us have fallen into the trap of being a lesser version of ourselves. Who hasn't walked away from a situation with regret biting at your heels, saying to yourself something along the lines of, 'What was I thinking?' or 'Why did I say that?' or (my personal favourite) 'Why did I have to be such a dick?'

Throughout the book I'll talk a lot about being a 'remarkable' colleague, leader, person and friend. So what is 'remarkable'? It is most often used to mean extraordinary, exceptional, amazing, wonderful or sensational. Getting to this level often seems near impossible. Being remarkable 100 per cent of the time is impossible. We just need to ask our spouse, parents, kids or close friends to know this is true. Aiming for perfection is not really good for us, so being remarkable, all the time, can seem an unreasonable quest.

What I am talking about when I refer to someone as remarkable is, *remark-able*— as in, that person is so good, in the way they communicate and collaborate, that people can't stop remarking on them, talking about them, referring to them. If we find something remarkable it means we want to talk about it, and in a good way. Being remarkable is the opposite of being a dick.

So how can we recognise those 'opposite' people? Those who are not impressive, amazing or sensational? Some of the obvious clues are when they:

- have too many wines at work functions and lose all ability to operate a moral compass
- give loud feedback across the open-plan office
- bark orders to people around them (especially to people they consider 'under' them)
- call their colleagues losers
- simply can't stop telling others why they are so awesome.

Unfortunately it's more common than not. And being unremarkable is not just about the obvious scenarios. There are also those who:

- don't speak up when someone needs defending
- avoid giving feedback to their team members so they are not given the opportunity to improve
- speak poorly of others behind their backs

- don't do what they say they are going to
- ask for your opinion but never heed your advice
- negotiate poor deals with customers for fear of losing them.

Unremarkable behaviour is anything that pushes people away from communicating and collaborating well with others.

I've researched the stats on disengaged employees. I was once an accountant, and I am fully aware of the costs to individuals and organisations. I've seen the impacts that unremarkable people have. It's not pretty, and unfortunately so many people accept it as the norm. 'Dicks are everywhere', people say with a sigh and resignation, or in frustration and pain.

THE IMPLICATIONS OF BEING A DICK

We will look at the costs and impacts for organisations in the next chapter but firstly is it important to understand the effect that being a dick has on the people around us, and on our ability to inspire and lead others.

- *Dicks are people we avoid.* They push others away with their actions, their inactions or their words. They may not be included in emails, meetings, social gatherings, or asked their opinions and ideas. They may not be aware they are being bypassed, but they are.

- *Dicks are people we don't trust or respect.* Their lack of interest or excessive self-interest, lack of rapport and lack of compassion does not engender trust and respect. It has the opposite effect. When people don't respect you or trust you, good luck building meaningful and fruitful relationships.

(continued)

THE IMPLICATIONS OF BEING A DICK (CONT'D)

- *Dicks are people that don't make the best decisions.* If they think their idea is the best idea, they pretend to include others in decision-making. If their knowledge makes them the only expert, expect flawed decision-making. After all, their truth is only one side of the story; it needs to be combined with other people's truths before the 'real truth' emerges.

- *Dicks are people that find it difficult to influence others.* The lack of inclusion, respect and compassion they demonstrate means it becomes difficult to inspire and influence others. If you can't influence others to get things done, it makes doing your job feel like pushing shit up a hill.

- *Dicks are people that push others away.* Whether they are aware of it or not, they repel others from collaborating and really connecting. When people are focused on themselves first and foremost they can push people away with their directness, 'rightness' and need to win. It comes at a cost.

- *Dicks are people at all levels.* Many people presume that being more senior, continuing to get promotions or being known for their expertise means that they must be remarkable. This is a big ego trap. There are plenty of unremarkable leaders at senior levels.

We've all worked with dicks, and if you are being honest and courageous you'll admit that you've also been one from time to time. I have been a dick at times. I wish I could turn back the clock. What I do know is that with the right self-awareness tools and regular practice, I get better every week, every month, every year. Just ask my friends and family (well, maybe not my ex). Mostly I'm improving. While this book is about tackling the arguably less complicated relationships (being those at work, rather than those close to home), the concepts, ideas and thinking all apply to both.

I could have called this book 'Your guide to becoming a remarkable communicator' or 'Fixing Feedback: Rewiring the workplace, people's mindsets and productivity', or 'iCommunication: Moving into 21st century communication for organisations and the people'. I don't know about you, but those titles make me sleepy. I've seen them before. I know the content. It's stiff and it's safe and it's stale.

Learning how to build remarkable relationships with people is not easy and it's not a matter of creating a checklist and ticking it off. It's a matter of learning not to *tick others off* by being a dick! It's about being open enough to become remarkable — so remarkable that people can't stop remarking on how enjoyable you are to work with, how they want to get on your projects and be on your team. Because they feel respected and heard. Because they feel valued and can see that they matter.

This book is a personal and professional treasure of insights created to educate you and your organisation about how to become remarkable, high-performing and seriously inspiring. Through giving great feedback and nailing the tough conversations, you can become a truly great person to work with; and by following the same principles, organisations can become truly great places to work.

So don't be a dick! Be remarkable!

Chapter 1
FEEDBACK IS BROKEN

In order to deal with people and issues at work we need to communicate. That means having conversations. You can't do a remarkable job without having remarkable conversations. You can't have remarkable relationships without having remarkable conversations.

New York Times bestseller *The 4-Hour Workweek* by Tim Ferriss suggests that we can structure our lives to be successful and wealthy by only working four hours a week—it is all about spending your time wisely. Ferriss says that 'a person's success in life can be measured by the number of uncomfortable conversations he or she is willing to have'. I agree with Ferriss that pushing through your fears and doing the tough stuff is all about getting things done and moving forward. I don't think it needs to be uncomfortable though. There is an easier way.

It's all about your people

You may know them as high-performing organisations, the best places to work, or employers of choice. Whatever you want to call them, all top organisations are similar in that they each recognise the power of creating and sustaining great cultures, and the power of communicating and collaborating well. They know that their main competitive edge is not their products or services. It's their people. The people behind what they deliver. It's the people that design and make or break the next strategy. It's the people that create motivation and drive within the organisation. It's the people, people, people!

Fail to acknowledge people and you're deluding yourself (and doing them a disservice).

Think of the commonalities shared by top organisations with enormous reach. Without an incredible team of innovators, Apple would not be able to launch the Apple Watch or the next iPhone. Facebook would not be able to create such a socially engaging and addictive platform. Without remarkable people behind the scenes Virgin Galactic would not be taking people to space.

Ideas don't create themselves, nor do they implement themselves. Of course most projects have spokespeople and lead directors who drive the vision, marketing and 'selling' as they go, but they have a team behind them. Without that team, there's nothing to market or sell.

It's easy to join the dots and say that making the most of your people should be a priority: focus on your people and the business will flourish. But employers can easily lose sight of their people, especially in times of economic stress.

In the 1990s I joined an entrepreneurial, forward-thinking and fast-growing business, HR and recruitment firm Morgan and Banks. One of the largest firms of its kind in the world, Morgan and Banks led from the front in terms of innovation and development. It was workplace utopia. I was in my early twenties and had lots of enthusiasm but little experience. Little did I realise how lucky I was. Whenever I catch up with colleagues from that time we always look back nostalgically. We worked our butts off, we made good money, we loved what we did and we had a ball working with each other. It was like the gold rush days for the corporates.

Geoff Morgan, one of the cofounders, was known for understanding and verbalising the fact that Morgan and Banks's assets (its people) were going up and down the lifts all day. Andrew Banks, the other cofounder, constantly drummed into us Peter Drucker's saying that 'culture eats strategy for breakfast'. These guys instinctively knew that the value of their business was their people and they invested in them heavily via fun and powerful inductions, pragmatic and engaging professional development, mentoring programs and annual all-of-business conferences.

After the business was sold, the focus shifted from the people to the numbers. The conversations and strategy became about needing to improve, grow, cut back, double. We were not used to this. We were used to being asked how to build capability and motivation. Unsurprisingly, productivity decreased and maintaining profits became a challenge. It became difficult to retain the star performers, and people left.

YOUR *people* ARE YOUR BIGGEST ASSETS. FOCUS ON THEM AND THE BUSINESS WILL PROSPER.

Too many companies still haven't figured out that if they want the customer to come first they need to focus on cultivating a happy workplace: it's your people who are dealing with the customers.

Zappos, the largest online shoe retailer in the world, prides itself on its company culture, and it is well known for it. Does it come as any surprise that 75 per cent of purchases are from returning customers? That's an amazing statistic and is part of the reason Zappos was able to grow so quickly. One of its core values is 'deliver WOW through service'. Zappos expects every employee to wow their customers and it does this by giving employees the autonomy to handle situations in any way they see fit.

Another organisation that is gaining more and more attention and success globally right now is Atlassian. Atlassian is a rapidly growing 'software loving' business that has won *Business Review Weekly*'s 'Best Place to Work' twice, along with over 50 other awards (including top 20 Fortune Company, Deloitte

Best Fast Growing IT and Hewitt's Best Employer) since it started in 2002. Even Dan Pink, author of the *New York Times* bestseller *Drive: The surprising truth about what motivates us*, uses Atlassian as an example in one of his famous TED talks. He says that Atlassian is an 'incredibly cool company' that is focused on motivating its people by giving them autonomy. Pink says too many organisations are basing their decisions on outdated thinking. If we want high-performance cultures the solution is not to entice employees with a sweeter carrot or a bigger stick.

With a dogged focus on values in everything it does with its employees, customers and brand, it's no wonder Atlassian has highly engaged people—and a very successful business with unprecedented growth in an arguably flat economy. It invests heavily in its people and sees the difference it makes. It's Atlassian's edge, and the results speak for themselves.

If we don't invest in our people and give them the feedback they need, we can't expect to have a high-performing business. People won't know what they need to replicate and what they need to improve.

People matter. A lot.

The people noise is loud

We need to get the best from our people so our businesses can thrive. So we get it, right?! Right!

Then why is it that some of the biggest problems we have in organisations are our people? People, our greatest treasure, can also become our greatest liability. 'People noise' can become so loud sometimes that it makes it hard to implement anything. People noise is like white noise … it's always on in the background until we turn it off.

When I say 'we' I don't mean us or them. I mean you. The leader, the manager, the colleague. If you see there is something to be done then *you* need to do it. We often wait for someone else to take the lead, have that conversation, or set the tone. No wonder it doesn't happen. As Gandhi said, 'Be the change that you wish to see in the world'.

MANAGERS NEED TO *manage*. MANAGING IS MORE ABOUT THE *people issues* THAN ANYTHING ELSE.

Peter Drucker tells us that most of what we call 'management' consists of making it difficult for people to get their work done. Managers either create the people noise themselves or they don't turn it off when they need to. They don't lead.

The issues that demand most of our time are often the people ones. Do any of these scenarios sound familiar?

- You are trying to prepare your weekly report and John pops in to discuss an issue he has with the project leader's style and how it is affecting the team.

- You are delivering a strategy that will improve the productivity of the business but Tom does not want to work with Mary to deliver it. She's just too difficult.

- You are leading Sam's performance review and giving him feedback on his consistently late delivery. You go into a battle about who needs to take responsibility, as he says Jennifer keeps holding him back.

- You want to implement a new system that will provide a smoother approach when working with clients, but half of the team is divided because they will be more dependent on IT and they don't enjoy working with that area of the business.

People noise is our constant whether we recognise it or not. The success of a great strategy and its implementation hinges on how well people work together. Harnessing this power as not just a manager, but as a 'doer', and reducing the people noise makes the process of working together easier and, dare I say, more enjoyable.

The eighth consecutive study on engagement conducted by research company Gallup tells us that the cost of disengaged employees is deemed critical to a company's performance. The statistics are highly compelling. Some examples of a highly engaged workforce where people enjoy coming to work and working with each other suggest that there is:

- 65 per cent less turnover
- 37 per cent less absenteeism
- 48 per cent fewer safety incidents.

It is clear that minimising the people issues and creating a highly engaged workforce makes a difference. We're not talking about satisfaction for its own sake. We are talking about the cost implications of not investing in your people. More about this in chapter 2.

There are three options for dealing with the people noise.

1 *Deal with people noise as it arises.* Nip it in the bud so the spot fires don't become bushfires that end up being overwhelming or near impossible to address.

2 *Deal with it poorly.* Create even more issues by tackling the problems improperly or incompletely, damaging trust and respect in the process through inappropriate or aggressive communication.

3 *Ignore them and hope they will go away.* I call managers who do this 'broken glass' managers: they step over the broken glass in the middle of the room in the hope that someone else will clean up the mess. Don't be a broken-glass manager. Get out the brush and shovel and deal with it.

Most managers pick option three and end up sweeping the glass shards under the carpet. The next group takes option two and 'attacks' the issue or person and deals with it poorly, only to see that the approach is ineffectual and often makes things worse. That is the behaviour of a dick.

Remarkable managers boldly tackle option one. They handle the complexities as they arise, with candour and kindness, and end up getting things done. People want to work for them.

Time poverty — a growing phenomenon

Time poverty is not having enough time to do all the things you want or need to do. Like a shortage of income, lack of time is a disadvantage for individuals and organisations.

Societally, we have never been busier. There is more to do, higher expectations that we will deliver it perfectly, and greater distraction from devices and social media than we've ever encountered in the past. There is increased competition in all aspects of products and services, ongoing family commitments, financial pressures in a challenged economy, and many people are facing technology overload. No wonder we feel time-poor.

The past ten years have given us a plethora of functional, fun and powerful electronic tools at our disposal. Many of them started out claiming to make our personal and working lives easier. There are electronic scheduling systems, handheld devices, and we have the ability to communicate with anyone, anywhere, at any time. Yet we still struggle to stay organised and focused. It's most likely due to the fact that we have more information to wade through than ever before. It all adds up to more excuses to not address problems when they happen, because we are 'busy' wading through our technology.

We are not leveraging technology

Productivity expert, thought leader and author of *Smart Work* Dermot Crowley says, 'We need more than just new technology to stay organised in the modern workplace. We need new mindsets, new systems and new skills'.

Crowley tells us that a large part of the problem is that we are using twenty-first century technologies, but still using twentieth-century methodologies. He says the main reasons we are so time-poor in this modern era are:

- *We have too many meetings, especially at the senior manager level.* It is not unusual for the modern

(continued)

we are not leveraging technology (cont'd)

manager to spend 80 per cent of their core hours in meetings. This leaves little time to read and respond to emails, solve issues, develop strategies and do the thinking to deliver the right outcomes. Weekends and late nights are often taken up getting to the other needs. We are not creating enough time to stop, think and plan.

- *We are drowning in emails.* Six years ago the average senior executive would have 60 emails per day to deal with. Now we are looking at an average of more than 300 per day. This email noise has created an unprecedented communications focus. These emails are a combination of cc's (copying people in), information only, marketing products and services, blogs, personal memos and event requests, just to name a few. No wonder important emails are sometimes hard to find.

- *Our use of technology is disabling our productivity.* While technology has made doing business and connecting with others easier it has also created a sense of urgency that is crippling the way we work. We can communicate with anyone at any time. This is generally seen as hugely advantageous, but it has also created a sense that everything is urgent and important. It is not the case: we just lack the tools and training to see what is urgent and what is important.

- *We procrastinate.* We need to relearn the art of planning what to do and committing to action. We put things off in the hope that they will go away or sort themselves out. It's no surprise they don't and then become much bigger than initially planned, and much more time-intensive—especially things like giving feedback and tackling tough conversations.

We need to learn to confront issues as soon as we see them. How many conversations with people—friends, colleagues and family—become more serious than they need to be because you don't 'nip them in the bud' in the early days? That is, when you first notice the issue or problem, or when something feels not quite right.

The things we let go vary widely: being spoken to rudely, observing someone arrive late, missing a deadline, or your manager cancelling your weekly catch-up again. It can be anything that seems small, at the time. You might decide it's not worth worrying about so you let it go because you 'don't sweat the small stuff', or because it has only happened once or twice and you are too nervous to approach the person. Perhaps you deny it will become something bigger, or perhaps you would just prefer to avoid conflict. There are plenty of reasons why we don't have the tough conversations but the point is, there is a downside to sticking your head in the proverbial sand.

Ignoring these issues can be the difference between dealing with a spot fire and fighting a raging bushfire. The longer we leave it the greater the costs to the business and ourselves.

When we see a spot fire we grab some water and put it out, right? We know that fire is dangerous and it could turn ugly pretty quickly. It's the same when we don't nip problems in the bud.

In 2014 McKinsey put out a white paper called 'Bad to Great: The path to scaling up excellence', which states that the most important factor in leadership excellence is the ability to 'nip it in the bud'. Leaders who are focused on improving behaviour improve organisational performance. Eliminating the negative is the first step in the process. Destructive behaviour—be it selfishness, nastiness, fear, laziness or dishonesty—packs a far bigger punch than constructive behaviour. Furthermore, it damages the bottom line.

Matrix structures add complexity

As organisations grow so do their complexities. In most organisations this leads to matrix structures, with people working on multiple projects across business lines, often with more than two managers.

About thirty years ago this structure became popular and organisations such as IBM, HP, Citibank, Nestle and Xerox led the way. Today it's not just for big businesses; many small to medium businesses are embracing it, too.

The purpose of these centralised and decentralised structures is to optimise productivity and rise to the modern challenges of managing virtual teams working on multiple projects across cross-functional and global platforms. These structures are also about responding to customers swiftly and efficiently.

For these matrix structures to work they need to be supported by the right structures and systems, plus a different way of managing and leading. Jay Galbraith, expert in matrix management, says in *Designing Matrix Organizations that Actually Work* that 'organization structures do not fail, but management fails at implementing them successfully'. Communication and cooperation are critical to the success of matrix structures, but managers and employees are not often taught how to work well in this environment and aren't equipped to communicate and collaborate effectively.

Think about it as being a bit like Heathrow, one of the busiest airports in the world. Processes and systems are essential but communication is considered an equal partner.

Most of the academic research into the success of matrix structures is not around the design but about the skills and behaviours needed to lead in these environments. Most of the disadvantages come from the way people work together—not from the structure.

Matrixes allow further internal complexities to develop across the silos. As we now have 'information silos' it can increase the layers of bureaucracy: more meetings and slower decision-making with too many stakeholders involved. This also creates more potential opportunities for internal conflict and results in too many cooks stirring the broth.

Having multiple managers creates confusion. Without enough communication it becomes hard to know what your priorities are as everything appears to be important. Who is your direct supervisor? Which project is the priority? When managers and teams are being pushed and pulled it becomes a battle of the fittest, and sometimes the loudest.

Getting control of your team is difficult, especially when you don't have face-to-face or even established relationships. Managers need to learn how to build trust in these situations in order to get things done.

It can be difficult to get an accurate picture of people's real performance. With dual managers it becomes hard for one manager to gather all the facts and information to deliver the most accurate and constructive feedback about performance.

This last point leads well into the next problem. It's one that organisations are aware of, but it is not often discussed or acknowledged.

Performance reviews are not working

'Wow! I'm so excited about my performance review.' Said no-one, ever.

For most people, performance reviews are as enticing as a trip to the dentist.

Why aren't they the tool for performance and development we need them to be? There are several reasons, but these are the main ones that I have observed over the past 20 years of leading and consulting to businesses.

- *The feedback is stale or hidden.* Most people want to avoid the tough conversations so they tend to store them up until the dreaded performance review. Many employers I've spoken to dislike performance reviews as much as their employees do. They become an excuse to avoid discussing things in the moment, as it happens. Or the feedback is delivered but it's hidden in the 'shit sandwich' of good point, bad point, good point. Or, worse still, it's mumbled haplessly in the hope that the full impact is uncovered from under the rock.

- *They are full of surprises, and not the good kind.* People tend to avoid tough conversations. Most people are naturally conflict-averse. What this means is that the initial issue presenting as a small problem can become an elephant in the room by the time the review comes around, and it may come as a complete surprise to the recipient. This causes all sorts of flow-on issues with trust and respect, as they were not told at the time, and this ends up having quite a negative impact overall.

- *There is little room for the 'real truth'.* The real truth is what one person knows *coupled with* what the other person knows. It is two perspectives that create the actual truth of a situation. The review process does not typically allow this to happen, as it is time-poor and 'tell' orientated. The numbers and results are typically decided prior to the review, so where is the 'real truth' in the process?

- *They highlight our crap.* While some organisations and managers have cottoned on to the power of building on strengths, unfortunately the majority still focus on an individual's skills gap as the main conversation. We only need to look at the work of Martin Seligman, a world leader in positive psychology, to understand that focusing on our weaknesses creates little chance of development and change. They need to be discussed, but not in the spotlight. They should be dealt with during the year.

- *They are too focused on scoring and box-ticking.* In larger organisations, managers typically need to grade you, sometimes on a scale of 1 to 5. We know that people will rarely get a 5, as this will mean an increase in salary or a big bonus. So while an employee might be doing really well, we don't want a budget crisis—so the scores don't truly reflect performance. Don't they say 'comparison is the killer of joy'? Well, here is a great example. How do you compare yourself to the next person? You can't and you shouldn't. Individuals are unique and have their own talents, so a box-ticking scale is pointless.

- *They are way too time-consuming.* Most managers have many performance reviews to prepare for and as a result it becomes about getting the job done rather than delivering in the best way possible. It can also build a little resentment in the process. There's no reward for all the invested time and effort when an employee is even further deterred from delivering good work.

- *They are stiff and boring.* Do you remember the feeling of going to your first school dance? How awkward it was in your first formal outfit, seeing your date look as uncomfortable as you but trying to pretend you are all just fine? Our reviews can be similar when they are too formal for any real discussion to take place.

The habit of having valuable conversations so people can be championed and supported to improve is a good thing. There is little evidence that the formal performance review process achieves this. In fact, most data suggests the contrary. Quality guru W. Edwards Deming was clearly against them, identifying 'evaluation of performance, merit rating, or annual review' as one of his Seven Deadly Diseases of Management.

Adobe, which produces software including Photoshop, Acrobat, Creative Cloud and the Digital Marketing suite, calculated that annual reviews required 80 000 hours of managers' time each year, the equivalent of 40 fulltime employees. And after all that effort, internal surveys revealed that employees felt less inspired and motivated, and staff turnover increased.

In 2012 the company was bold enough to make a change and got rid of formal appraisals in favour of creating regular 'pulse checks'. This affected 11 000 employees. Since implementing this change Adobe has reported a considerable shift in engagement, culture and productivity. Other reputable organisations have agreed that performance reviews are not working. Accenture, Microsoft, Deloitte and Expedia have all either moved away from the formal systems or made radical changes. Deloitte's research and costing tells us that an annual appraisal for 65 000 staff took 2 million hours. Expedia says it mostly wanted to 'rehumanise' the relationship between employees and bosses.

The Corporate Leadership Council (CLC) produced well-recognised findings in the paper 'Building the High-Performance Workforce'. CLC research tells us that the impact of informal feedback—that is, feedback outside a formal process that is fair and accurate—is likely to improve individual performance by almost 40 per cent. So if we give feedback on the job, near the moment, it will create a shift 40 per cent of the time. That's pretty compelling.

It's time to move to the future

Nelson Jackson was onto it when he said, 'I do not believe you can do today's job with yesterday's methods and be in business tomorrow'.

The concept of 'performance management' was introduced about sixty years ago as a means to determine the wages of an employee based on their performance. It was used to drive behaviours to generate specific outcomes. When employees were solely driven by financial rewards this tended to work well.

In the late 1980s not all employees felt rewarded or motivated by financial gain alone; many were driven by learning and the development of their skills. From here performance management started moving into more frequent monitoring and reviews with a focus on 'regular feedback' outside the formal review process. As organisations put more regular conversations into the mix there was a notable improvement in productivity and employee engagement, when the conversations were handled well.

We are now seeing an emerging trend in high-performing organisations where all employees, not just the leaders, are being taught how to give great feedback and also how to receive feedback with equal candour and grace. Organisations that do this are in their 'feedback flow', as shown in figure 1.1.

Figure 1.1: the feedback flow

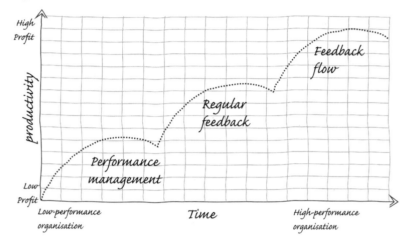

The concept of 'flow' proposed by Mihály Csíkszentmihályi, a well-known Hungarian psychology professor, is described as being a state in which motivation meets capability. In this space where you are driven to achieve (motivation) and your skills are at the right level (capability), you are in your flow. This creates energy and alignment with the tasks you are doing. It's where action and awareness meet. Flow is good.

Creating a feedback flow is how high-performing organisations get things done and create happy, fully engaged employees and customers. It is where we reverse the push of giving feedback and add to it the pull of receiving it, and alter systems to create an even flow.

So why don't organisations and leaders implement this powerful culture of feedback? There are three main reasons holding them back:

- Organisations don't muster the courage to invest in their people and culture. They are stuck in the 1940s and they just don't get it. As a result, these are not high-performing companies.

- Even for those that value and encourage feedback it is still not translating into action, or the actions are often damaging. The intent may be good, but intent is not seen or measured. We are still avoiding conversations or handling them poorly, no matter how much training we receive.

- People think the change will be too hard and too disruptive. Creating a cultural shift requires effort, but taking out a layer of processes and systems that use considerable time for little or no result will free up time to focus on actual improvement.

We often blame the organisation and its leaders for failures in feedback and get stuck in what I call 'the blame trap'. Getting stuck in the blame trap means we blame others, organisations and leaders and do not take any responsibility ourselves. It's not a healthy space, nor does it allow anyone to move forward.

Remarkable leaders

Leaders are not just those with impressive titles. They are not just those who manage people or have lots of letters after their names. Yes, they may have people reporting to them. They may be in senior roles within an organisation, but they may not. Leadership is about social influence — being able to secure the support or assistance of other people in order to accomplish something. This description of leadership doesn't make reference to 'leading people' or 'being in a senior role'. Leadership is less about hierarchy and more about influencing others to get things done.

A leader can be someone who works in Accounts Payable who decides who gets paid and who doesn't and builds relationships with suppliers and internal colleagues in the process. A leader can be a product developer who deals with researchers, customers, IT, sales and other areas to come up with the best ideas and products to launch.

EVERYONE *works* WITH SOMEONE. EVERYONE *collaborates* WITH SOMEONE. EVERYONE *communicates* WITH SOMEONE. WE ARE ALL LEADERS. WE JUST DON'T ALWAYS SEE IT THAT WAY.

When you think about the structure of an organisation, those that lead people are the minority. While they occupy the top of the triangle they represent, their segment is the smallest part of the organisation. So if we arm only the leaders with the tools and training to become remarkable then we are missing a very large component of the business (and arguably one that will drive the most change). Everyone within an organisation needs to take responsibility, no matter what role they play.

Kerry Patterson, Joseph Grenny, Ron McMillan and Al Switzler, the authors of *Crucial Conversations* and the cofounders of VitalSmarts, conducted 25 years of research involving thousands of people and hundreds of organisations. The findings suggest that the most influential individuals are those who get things done, are able to build good relationships *and* master the tough conversations.

It is leaders (whether they manage people or not) who influence projects, thinking and the implementation of ideas. If you want to influence effectively, you need to become a leader.

The research looked at both high- and low-performing organisations. Typically, low-performing organisations ignored poor performers and had a workforce where people didn't hold each other accountable. Meanwhile, high-performing organisations tended to have a culture where managers dealt with issues as they arose and discussed problems before they flared up.

You may have heard the adage 'a fish rots from the head'. You can equate this to the leadership of a business. A business will rot if the leaders at the top are not inspiring, trustworthy, or strategic enough. So we do need to focus on them — but not in isolation. We need to focus on the other leaders in the business, too.

Everyone who connects with someone is a potential leader. So unless you are in an isolated basement, working on something that requires no interaction with anyone else, this is for you. Expecting others to change so that the culture can improve, without taking ownership yourself, is being a dick.

Just because you become a parent doesn't mean you are a good one. Just because you are a doctor and deal with people all day does not mean you have a great bedside manner. Just because you speak at functions does not mean you do it well. The same goes for leadership. Just because you lead people or projects does not mean you influence people well. We need to learn to develop the talent and skills of leading remarkably, and having the tough conversations, so things get done with ease and enjoyment.

Gandhi knew this when he said: 'I suppose leadership at one time meant muscles; but today it means getting along with people'. Bill Gates knows it too: 'As we look ahead into the next century, leaders will be those who empower others'.

Everyone needs to lead the charge when it comes to influencing outstanding cultures and change. You don't fight a war with only the leaders equipped with armour and weapons, so why would you assume that only leaders need to be remarkable? It's impossible to win the battle without everyone taking up arms..

Fixing feedback

Fixing feedback is about creating a cultural cadence. It's more than feedback training. It's about creating a self-sustaining flow that feeds itself and becomes effortless. The onus is on both parties: one to deliver the feedback, in real time, and the other to receive it well, in the moment. The outcomes of this will:

- eliminate dependence on performance management systems
- significantly improve productivity
- create a culture of accountability and commitment
- evolve authentic transparency and openness
- allow individuals to own their own development.

When we create a frequency of accountability that feeds itself, giving and receiving becomes an inevitable part of the way you do business. You *and* the organisation are in your flow. You and your people become remarkable and no-one can stop talking about it.

YOUR CHEAT SHEET

- You can't do a remarkable job without having remarkable conversations.

- All top organisations are similar in that they each recognise the power of creating and sustaining great cultures, and the power of communicating and collaborating well.

- The success of a great strategy and its implementation hinges on how well people work together.

- Remarkable managers deal with issues as they arise, and end up getting things done.

- We need to learn to confront issues as soon as we see them. The longer we leave them the greater the costs to the business and ourselves.

- Communication and cooperation are critical in complex structures, but people are often not equipped to communicate and collaborate effectively.

- There is little evidence that formal performance reviews work. The habit of having regular and constructive conversations is key.

- In many high-performing organisations all employees, not just the leaders, are being taught how to give great feedback and how to receive it.

- Leadership is about influence. The most influential individuals are those who get things done, are able to build good relationships *and* master the tough conversations.

Chapter 2

THE COST OF POOR COMMUNICATION

Building trust and respect in the workplace is a significant contributor to high performance in an organisation. The better the relationships, the more productive the workplace. We've heard it before. We know it!

When conversations matter we often do our worst. We make a poor effort or a damaging attempt—or we avoid them altogether and this becomes the norm. After all, the issue will just go away won't it? No. It won't. The effect is that employees become disengaged, and that always has its own consequences.

As long as the job gets done, does employee engagement really matter? Turns out it does, and much more than we care to acknowledge.

In 2012 the research group Gallup conducted an extensive study into the effect of employee engagement. They looked at almost 50 000 businesses, nearly 1.5 million employees in 34 countries, and discovered the organisations that score in the top 50 per cent for employee engagement have *double* the odds of success of those in the bottom 50 per cent. Not only that, but those workplaces in the 99th percentile of engagement have *four times* the success rate.

COMMUNICATION IS LIKE *money*. YOU CAN NEVER HAVE ENOUGH.

This is the eighth year Gallup has done a study such as this, and the results have been remarkably consistent each time. And if you are interested in seeing the bottom line when it comes to low employee engagement, then there's some pretty compelling data to look at.

High employee engagement is actually critical to a company's performance. According to Gallup, high levels of engagement affect 10 key performance outcomes:

- 37 per cent lower absenteeism
- 25 per cent lower employee turnover (in high-turnover organisations)
- 65 per cent lower employee turnover (in low-turnover organisations)
- 28 per cent less shrinkage
- 48 per cent fewer safety incidents
- 41 per cent fewer patient safety incidents
- 41 per cent fewer quality incidents (defects)
- 10 per cent higher customer metrics
- 21 per cent higher productivity
- 22 per cent higher profitability.

Table 2.1 shows the ways in which poor engagement affects an organisation. It's just so important for employees to feel seen and connected to the organisation and the people they are working with. The aim is to move them up the ladder, from a position of disregarding their workplace and the people around them (which results in sabotage and significant losses) to a position of being devoted (which results in a workforce that is effortless to lead and creates significant profitability for the business).

Table 2.1: the impact of poor engagement

Individual engagement	Workplace results	Effect on productivity
Devoted	Effortless	+100
Dedicated	Discretionary	+50
Committed	Compliance	+10
Tolerant	Non-committal	−10
Withdrawn	Pollution	−50
Disregard	Sabotage	−100

According to a study by human resources software company BambooHR, while younger people are annoyed by low salaries, salary becomes less important to employees as they age. They found that the real deal-breakers are issues with bosses and coworkers and a skewed work–life balance.

Additionally, according to a Gallup poll of more than a million employed Americans, a bad boss or supervisor is the number one reason people leave. If the workplace environment is poor and they feel they've been treated badly, people tend to vote with their feet.

And if you're not convinced yet, Leigh Branham, author of *The 7 Hidden Reasons Employees Leave: How to Recognize the Subtle Signs and Act Before It's Too Late*, says that while most people tell human resources they are leaving for more money or a better opportunity, it's usually not the truth. Almost 90 per cent change jobs because of issues they have with the workplace, which can be anything from substandard management to a noxious culture.

Good strategy is nothing without good people. Moving your business forward relies on people working together. Great communication needs great conversations, which in turn create accelerated communication.

BaD BeHaviour is expensive

We've all come across dysfunctional and unproductive behaviour in the workplace, but the results of a study by SACS Consulting suggest that the problem might be more widespread than you'd think. Of the more than 1000 Australian professionals surveyed, two-thirds admitted to behaviours such as taking sick leave when they're not ill, being intentionally rude—and even stealing from the workplace.

No dollar figure has been placed on the cost of bad work behaviours in Australia, but in the US it's estimated at about $4.2 billion per year—and that's just the financial cost.

B2B needs more H2H

When thinking about customers, whether they be businesses or consumers, we are all trying to build outstanding strategies, systems, processes and operations to connect and impress. The business (B2B) stuff. But in the process we are missing what makes these outstanding—having *remarkable* communications with *the people* behind those strategies, systems, processes and operations.

We're not talking about 'how was your weekend?' We're talking about real, honest, difficult, challenging conversations, or feedback moments. Those moments that make things happen *and* improve trust and respect in the process. The human-to-human (H2H) stuff.

We're not focusing enough on the very thing that makes the biggest difference: collaboration ... through conversations ... with people! Focusing on strategy alone is like a scientist working on a vaccine without understanding what the market really needs and wants. It's just inefficient and ineffective.

When we move from isolation (creating B2B ideas and strategies in our own little team silos) to collaboration (H2H) we improve profits and dramatically improve service and delivery.

Perhaps we can learn from Yves Morieux from BCG, an impressive global consulting firm. Morieux researches how corporations can adapt within modern and complex business landscapes. He says that 'when people cooperate you need less resources'. Imagine if every car manufacturer, when designing its 'new and improved' car, collaborated authentically with the service team to ensure the maintenance issues were minimised and the car became even more responsive? Costs would reduce as repairs decreased, the marketing sell would become more powerful, and we would have better relationships with people across the business and be better able to get more things done in the future: H2H at its best, right there. When people collaborate effectively, and respectfully, it creates a higher level of productivity and results in smarter decisions for the business.

Jimmy Wales, the cofounder of Wikipedia, learned that 'things work well when a group of people know each other, and things break down when it's a group of random people interacting'.

I work with many technology businesses so I was particularly interested to see an article in *CIO Magazine* that mentioned the secret weapon that great CIOs possess is good communication skills. This means picking up the phone or walking over and having a face-to-face talk.

This H2H approach should also extend to our interactions with customers. There are many tough conversations we need to be having with customers, such as saying no to impossible requirements or letting a client know we will not be able to meet deadlines. There is a way to have those conversations that engenders trust and respect rather than damaging it. See chapter 5 for details.

Mike Rutherford, a musician from the UK, put it so well when he said: 'Being in a band is always a bit of a compromise... provided the balance is good, what you lose in compromise you gain ... by the collaboration'. So if we know that collaboration, through great conversations with each other and our customers, creates our competitive edge, then let's get some more H2H in our B2B.

YOUR CHEAT SHEET

- Collaboration, through great conversations with each other and our customers, creates our competitive edge. It is one of the main levers to grow engagement in any organisation.

- Employee engagement really does matter. It's critical to a company's performance.

- Choosing not to focus on this is costly for your business and its people

- Strategies, systems, processes and operations become remarkable when there's remarkable communication between the people creating them.

- It's the human-to-human (H2H) stuff that improves the B2B (business-to-business) growth.

- Real, honest, difficult, challenging conversations, or feedback moments, are what make things happen and improve trust and respect in the process.

Chapter 3

WHY DON'T WE HAVE THE CONVERSATION?

We've seen in the first two chapters how vital it is to become remarkable communicators, and that the responsibility lies with all of us. That's not so hard to connect with in our heads, but it can be difficult to put into practice. This is why so many of us still avoid tough conversations, or make a mess of them and walk away with 'regretitis'. Regretitis is a disease I have come across way too often — in my own life and in other people's. It makes you relive the conversation over and over again in your head, thinking about all the things you could and should have said ... or not said.

Avoiding a conversation that needs to be had is like sticking your head in the sand. We tend to think that conflict is unhealthy because we find it impossible to marry candour with kindness. The good news is that there is a way.

What's stopping you from delivering or receiving remarkable feedback? Have you ever:

- told a 'white lie' or exaggerated or downplayed information to prove your point or get your idea over the line

- delivered feedback that was harsh and damaging (but you were 'just being honest')

- avoided giving well-delivered feedback that would have benefited someone else because you wanted to avoid conflict

- started or participated in gossip that could have been (or was) damaging to a colleague

- not been honest with a colleague in a meeting or conversation, in order to avoid conflict

- not received feedback well from a colleague, because you don't respect them or value their thinking

- been remiss in giving a colleague or team member praise and/or recognition for a job well done

- not been open enough to someone else's point of view, for whatever reason?

Of course you have!

In every program I ask this question to the client and the participants: Why do we avoid or handle feedback and tough conversations so poorly? I hear nearly the same answers every time, irrespective of the industry, the experience or the seniority of the group. We all struggle with the same stuff. There is some comfort in this.

Reasons for avoiding feedback conversations (or having them poorly)

- *It's easier to do the task myself.* This is the excuse we give ourselves. When we do things ourselves we miss opportunities to teach and reset expectations.

- *I've already made my expectations clear.* We think we have been clear about what is expected, or we assume that it is common sense. Either way, it's not working.

- *It will pass.* We live and wait in hope that the issue will miraculously disappear.

- *They know how I feel.* Pulling a disappointment face doesn't change behaviour.

- *It will become an argument.* We want to avoid conflict at all costs even when those costs include poor results or behaviour. Having a 'he said she said' conversation is the last thing we want.

- *It will demotivate them or they will leave.* Unfortunately this is a common reason for avoiding tough conversations with those 'high performers'. We don't want to rock the boat because we might lose a large revenue generator or a project lead.

- *I don't want to be seen as a micromanager.* We are more worried about our reputation than about holding others to account.

- *It might ruin the relationship.* The last thing we want to do is damage the relationship. The fact is, we damage it with inaction anyway.

- *I don't have the confidence.* Not everyone is wired to feel bold and courageous enough to tackle difficult conversations.

- *I'm not sure how to approach it.* It's all well and good to know that something needs to be said, but how the heck do you structure it?

- *It's not my job/not my team member.* The old 'someone else should tell them' chestnut. The new school of leadership dictates that if you see an issue then you need to have the conversation.

- *I don't have time.* There is a myth that it will end up taking too much time. Just wait until the spot fire has become a bushfire and you'll realise how much more time and resources it will take to fix then.

- *There's no point. Nothing will change.* This is not an uncommon sentiment, and it gives people a feeling of helplessness. Perhaps we didn't tackle it well enough the other times?

Resonate with many of these? I expect you will. The good news is that you are not alone. Most people, without the right training and development, struggle in this space. Yet it's the toughest conversations that often create the biggest shifts.

What are *those* conversations?

Some feedback conversations can be simple and some more difficult, yet we avoid them for the same reasons.

What makes feedback conversations so difficult?

- *The relationship is poor.* When there's no (or little) trust or respect for one or both parties then we are less likely to have the conversation or to care about the impact. So we avoid or don't take responsibility for the outcomes (or lack thereof).

- *They trigger our emotions.* Whether it's the content, the person or the issue we, or they, have an emotional reaction—the more aggressive, the more obvious. One or both parties could be angry, teary, frustrated, annoyed or upset. Even for those who react quietly, the emotions are still there. The reaction does not have to be dramatic or overt to count.

- *You may disagree.* If we all agreed with each other, no matter what we said or how we said it, then there would be no need for this book. However, it is only in disagreement that we can challenge and push the status quo. This is how innovation occurs. Most people don't see things this way. When people do not agree things often get uncomfortable. It becomes personal.

- *The impact is significant.* The outcome or potential impact has weight for one or both parties. The impact could be potentially losing your job, losing a friend, not getting that raise you were hoping for, or having your ego or sense of self challenged. They all count.

We have three choices when it comes to having tough conversations.

1 We can put our head in the sand and avoid them.

2 We can tackle them and do damage in the process.

3 We can have them and have them well.

My passion and business is built on number 3. It makes such a big difference. It's time to tackle these conversations rather than hiding behind our excuses. Otherwise nothing will change.

Not all feedback is helpful

There is a difference between good feedback and poor feedback.

THE GOOD NEWS IS THAT *positive* FEEDBACK IS PROVEN TO DRIVE MORE POSITIVE CHANGE AND *performance* THAN THE NEGATIVE.

Researcher Marcial Losada has found that among high-performing teams in the workplace, the expression of positive feedback outweighs that of negative feedback by a ratio of nearly 6 to 1. By contrast, in low-performing teams the ratio is about 1.4 to 1.

The Corporate Leadership Council paper 'Building the High-Performance Workforce' gives similarly powerful data: when leaders focus on improving people's strengths they are about 36 per cent more likely to improve performance. Compare this to when leaders place emphasis on an employee's weaknesses: they actually create a negative shift in performance by nearly 27 per cent.

This means that people who want to create a highly productive and thriving team need to get good at giving positive feedback at least four times more often than they give constructive feedback. This is contrary to what many of us believe. After all, it's all about improving our weakness, closing the gaps and lifting our game, right?! Well, yes and no.

The research tells us that if you let people know what they are doing well, then they are likely to repeat the desired behaviours faster and better than if you focus on weaknesses alone. It's about how we are motivated to change. It's not just applicable at work, either. We can use this same concept at home.

When I tell my daughter how impressed I am that she apologises when she has been in the wrong and that it is a show of great strength of character, what is likely to happen in the future? Yes, she is likely to (and does) offer apologies when they are deserved. If I told her how poor she is at apologies then the behaviour change would be less likely. Similarly, I let my colleagues and clients know how much I value them getting back to me promptly with emails or phone calls. And surprise, they either get even better or continue to be consistent. (Not all the time, but mostly.)

It's not just the volume of positive to negative feedback that we often get wrong; it's also the quality. There is a difference between constructive feedback that drives change and the other form, which is praise or criticism that is not helpful and can be damaging.

Feedback that improves performance, drives change and is easily understood and learned from sits in the top row of table 3.1. It is specific and based on tangible observations. The bottom row of table 3.1 is what we want to avoid: praise and criticism are opinions or vague statements.

Table 3.1: feedback quality and impact

	Positive	Negative	
High impact	**Constructive feedback— positive** • Information-specific, issue-focused, and based on observation • About an effort well done • Objective, specific and non-judgemental • Not about 'right' or 'wrong', so it encourages discussion	**Constructive feedback— negative** • Information-specific, issue-focused, and based on observation • About an effort that needs improvement • Objective, specific and non-judgemental • Not accusing— focused on outcomes	*High impact*
Low or damaging impact	**Praise** • Personal and favourable judgement • General and vague • Doesn't encourage discussion, so can come across as hollow, insincere or lacking in substance • Based on opinions and feelings	**Criticism** • Personal and unfavourable judgement • General and vague • Not specific, so can lead to a battle over whose perception is 'right' or 'wrong' • Based on opinions and feelings	*Low or damaging impact*

Here are some examples of what these different types of feedback might look like:

'Positive'

- 'I really like how you listen clearly, respond to the brief and meet your deadlines' (constructive feedback—positive)
- 'I really like working with you' (praise)

The first statement tells me what I am doing that makes me good to work with. The second statement leaves me in the dark.

'Negative'

- 'A couple of people have mentioned that they struggle with your leadership when you don't hold their colleagues to account, don't have the tough conversations and address behavioural issues. For example ...' (constructive feedback—negative)
- 'People don't rate your leadership style' (criticism)

The first statement tells me what I am doing that makes people struggle with my leadership style, and concrete examples help me to put it in context. The second statement leaves me in the dark (and probably very defensive).

* * *

So we know we avoid the tough conversations. And that when we do have them they can be ineffective or damaging. We have learned that this costs the business and the culture and can damage trust and respect in the process.

But it's hard, right?! It is when we don't know how to do it well. When we are shown the tools and techniques to do it well, and we put them into action, people and workplaces transform. And here's the good news: it's not as hard as you think.

YOUR CHEAT SHEET

- We tend to avoid the tough conversations, or feedback moments, and we are not alone. Giving and receiving feedback can be difficult.

- When we do approach them we may do it poorly and damage relationships in the process.

- Constructive feedback that is based on evidence and examples drives performance. Praise and criticism do not.

- We need to get our positive on. High-performing organisations give four times more positive constructive feedback than constructive negative feedback.

- It's not just the quantity of feedback but the quality that makes the difference.

Chapter 4

UNDERSTANDING THE 'REAL TRUTH'

I have learned two very important techniques over the years when delivering feedback. First, the content needs to be delivered with facts—not your opinions or feelings (which are often the damaging pieces). Second, it is not *what* you say but *how* you say it that can make the difference. The difference between something said in frustration and with accusation, versus the same thing said tentatively and with compassion, is enormous.

In this chapter we examine the importance of presenting the real facts without the loaded opinion.

Honesty versus verbal assassination

Do you stand behind 'I'm just being honest' as an excuse to verbally assassinate someone? Have you seen others do this? Have you been on the receiving end? Unfortunately, you are likely to answer yes to at least one of these questions.

You're in a performance review and your manager tells you that a couple of your colleagues think your ego walks in the door two hours before you do. It's okay though, because he's 'just being honest'.

You're having a discussion with a colleague and she raises her voice, points her finger and lets you know that 'you should keep your mouth shut unless someone asks for your opinion'. It's okay though, because she's 'just being honest'.

Then there's this one, one of my favourites, which happened to a good friend of mine. He had just finished a finely tuned speech that he had been preparing for weeks and someone he knew came up to him after and said: 'That's the first time you have spoken and I haven't wanted to slap you'. It's okay though, because she was 'just being honest'.

Those four words 'I'm just being honest' seem to give some people permission to say whatever they think. After all, we live in a world of free speech. But there are serious consequences to saying whatever we think. Not only does the trust and respect bank get depleted but the 'discretionary effort' bank does too. We don't want to go the extra distance for these people, whether they be friends or colleagues, anymore. Engagement drops because they have hurt us. And we might believe the 'truth' they have presented to us, or go into a downward emotional spiral.

We've all worked with abrasive people. Laura Crawshaw, founder of the US-based Boss Whispering Institute, says there are two types of abrasive leaders:

1 those with a mental disorder

2 those with a moral disorder.

So why would anyone choose to grind another person's self-esteem down to the size of a pea? There are many reasons, and they're often bedded deep down. People are complicated beings. It can be their need to control, their need to feel bigger or more important than those around them, or it could be that intimidation has been a strong part of their upbringing. Whatever the reason, it's not just their moral compass they need to take ownership of; they also need to understand the impact they have on others. When we speak, our words can harm our colleagues, and we create an emotional wake ... whether we like it or not.

Opinions are not facts

One of the most important factors in giving feedback is learning to separate the facts from your opinions and feelings. Facts are non-disputable pieces of information. They can be proven, are measurable, precise and filled with exact information. While your feelings and opinions are true for *you*, they are not the absolute truth. If someone can argue with your 'facts' then they are not facts.

It's easy to understand that when we open our conversations with our 'truths' that are just loaded opinions and feelings, the other person is not going to effectively take the new information on board. An easy way to spot opinions and feelings is that they are often loaded as absolutes, such as 'no-one enjoys working with you' or 'everybody says you don't respect them'. The statements might reflect what you believe but rarely do they reflect what the whole workforce believes. It's safe to say that statements like these are not the way to begin a productive conversation. Nor are they facts.

I was recently coaching a marketing director with more than 20 years' experience in leading business units and people. He was easy to build rapport with and was very passionate about his work and his team. He had a number of 'underperforming' leaders. He had had the tough conversations with them several times. He'd let them know that there was a problem and that there would be repercussions if they did not improve. In his words, he had been brave enough to be honest and he had delivered the feedback with empathy and respect, but still they were not improving. I asked him what he had told them. He said, 'I told them that they were not performing to the standard set by the organisation. I said they needed to improve in order to keep their jobs or we would have to go down a formal performance management process. A path I did not want to go down with them'.

'What else?' I asked. 'Nothing else. That was clear enough.'

So. How did they respond?

The first leader agreed and thanked him for the feedback. The second got defensive, and suggested the marketing director have a look at his own performance before reprimanding others. (That conversation did not end well.) The third leader wanted examples and was really surprised and offended that she had not been told earlier. To be honest, I would have felt the same.

So I asked the marketing director what the facts were. He told me they were not performing to the level they should be. 'What level?' I asked. 'What exactly should they be doing? When did they underperform and what are the examples? What were they being measured against? How would they know this? What did they say or do that was not up to the standards?'

While the marketing director may have had good rapport with his leaders, he did them no favours by talking to them about his opinion of their performance. Yes, in his opinion they were not performing. While it might have been true, it is never helpful to lead the conversation with this. People need to know the facts—the tangible, un-arguable, proven truths that they cannot refute (for example, the dates they did not submit their reports on time, the budgets they did not meet, the people in their team that are not performing and why, the poor feedback from their customers).

If you lead with opinions then you should expect poor outcomes, poor performance and poor relationships. People need facts to hang on to so they can understand exactly what is not working, or what needs improvement. They don't need your thoughts about it.

Speculation kills outcomes

Speculation is when we spend time thinking about something that may or may not be true. It's when we ponder or make a decision about a situation or relationship based on *our* perspective of the facts, or *our* opinions of the facts.

We then speculate on our opinions and feelings, tell ourselves a story about the situation or person and lead with that story when giving the feedback. For example, your colleague Sarah has turned up late for the last three team meetings. In this case, the facts would be the actual times and dates she was late. Your opinion is that Sarah does not respect other people's time. So you tell yourself that Sarah does not respect your role as her manager. Then, when giving Sarah the feedback you lead with the story that she does not respect you ... So, how well do you think that conversation will go?

Deciding how the other person is thinking or feeling is another clear case of speculation. We decide they have an attitude problem, or we decide that our colleague does not like us, or that our team member is not invested enough in the outcomes. What we don't know is what they *are* thinking and feeling, until we ask them. (And even then we might not be presented with the truth.)

The way we interpret situations, people and data is based on our cognitive distortions. We judge people, situations and information according to what we see and what we believe. We base our judgements on our perspectives, which can be incorrect. There's more on this in chapter 7.

Opinions and feelings that are unhelpful, negative and not known to be true end up warping conversations and stunting communications. The story we tell ourselves typically becomes the story we lead a conversation with, or the story we ruminate on and fill our minds with. There are lots of problems with using 'the story we tell ourselves' to lead a feedback conversation.

1   We have assumed we know how someone thinks and feels.

2   We do not present the facts or ask for their thoughts in order to understand their side.

3   Leading with a false story damages trust and respect in the relationship.

4   It is likely the conversation could go south very quickly because of our preconceived story.

5   We have led ourselves into an unhealthy and often incorrect thinking trap.

The following examples might help to illustrate how quickly we lead with opinions and stories:

Example 1: A colleague cancels meetings with you on a regular basis. You then speculate that your colleague does not want to work with you, or that they don't respect your time, or that your colleague is incompetent.

All we know at this stage is the fact that you have had x number of meetings cancelled on x days. The rest is speculation.

> *Example 2:* Your manager cuts you off in a meeting with a customer. You speculate that your job is on the line, that the customer has told your manager they don't want to work with you, or that your manager doesn't value your input.

Aside from the fact that your manager cut you off by saying x, the rest is speculation.

LEADING YOUR CONVERSATION WITH 'THE STORY' IS AS *helpful* AS DRIVING A CAR BLINDFOLDED. IT'S GOT *crash* WRITTEN ALL OVER IT.

Figure 4.1 shows that speculation and story have no place in remarkable conversations. We need to learn to gather the facts, separate the opinions and feelings, and remove the story we are telling ourselves. Facts don't damage relationships and outcomes. They are the foundations of the discussion. We need to stop once we gather the facts so that speculation doesn't ruin the chance for a positive outcome.

Figure 4.1: speculation killed the cat

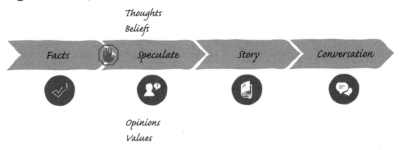

'Don't jump to conclusions. There may be a perfectly good explanation for what you just saw.' Proverbs 25:8 taught us this thousands of years ago—it is not new thinking. It's time to get a handle on it, though, and see the damaging repercussions that forming conclusions without facts has on relationships and outcomes.

Ruminating all over yourself

I had dinner with a friend and a couple of things were said that just didn't sit right at the time. You know that feeling where your gut reacts and you know you have to breathe, to calm your reaction down, before you even consider speaking? I knew that I needed to go away and process what I was thinking before deciding what to do with the way I was feeling. In the past I've acted out how I was feeling in the moment, and most of the time it did not serve me well.

Man oh man, did I milk the hell out of that conversation in my head. I thought about every possible reason for my friend saying what she said. From childhood issues, to exhaustion, lack of self-awareness, and selfishness, I then started to think that perhaps I was overreacting, or projecting my stuff. Maybe I needed to take a good look at myself and stop being so hard on others? But then I swung back to thinking that my friend needed to learn about the impact of the way she connects, and then I swung back to me and what a judgemental friend I am.

I regurgitated this conversation, and all the potential reasons for it, over and over again in my head for way, way too long. Then, of course, what happened? It became a *thing*. Because I spent so much time thinking about all the same possibilities over and over and over again, it became all-consuming.

I call this type of thinking 'ruminating all over yourself'. There is actually a condition called 'rumination syndrome' which is a medical condition described as 'the effortless regurgitation of meals after consumption'. I have taken artistic licence and will use it in this context and suggest it is 'the effortless regurgitation of thoughts after a conversation or situation'.

On average we have 50000 thoughts per day. On average, 95 per cent of the things you think about every day are the same thoughts, maybe disguised with different variations, but essentially the same. Of those 95 per cent of thoughts, generally 80 per cent of them are negative. They're not good for you and don't serve you well. That's some interesting data.

So, we ruminate on the same thoughts over and over, and most of them are detrimental to ourselves, our relationships and ultimately to the way we connect with others. We tend to let things fester, even when they are not even correct. They are mostly based on our feelings and opinions and speculations—not on the facts.

For many of us, the person we trust the most in our world is...ourselves. So if this is the case and we ruminate on mostly negative thoughts, then what happens when we speak negatively, punish or talk down to ourselves?

Yes, we can get lost in anxiety, frustration, blame and resentment. We might lose our confidence, kill our self-esteem or end up in the wrong places—or even in the wrong conversations—because we let things fester.

RUMINATING ON THE SAME *thoughts* OVER AND OVER AGAIN IS LIKE BEING ON A *merry-go-round* AND NOT BEING ABLE TO GET OFF.

Practising the process of killing the ANTs is a good start. ANTs are Automatic Negative Thoughts. They will come, whether or not you meditate, do yoga or keep yourself stupidly busy. You have no choice. But you do have a choice between accepting them and killing them.

So all this is really important to know, but why is it relevant? If more than three-quarters of our thoughts are negative, and these are the thoughts we focus on, we need to be careful not to speculate, or tell ourselves an incorrect story. Especially not a story we lead with when we are in a conversation or feedback moment.

Figure 4.2 shows the vicious cycle of thinking that launches us into negative emotions and then poor reactions.

Figure 4.2: the negativity roundabout

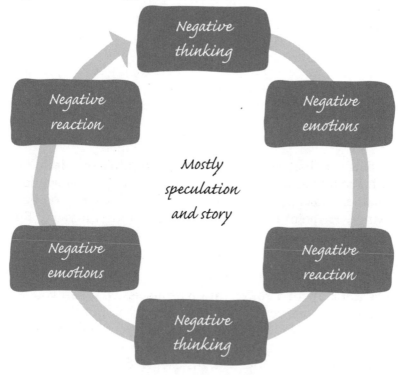

At what stage should you decide to stop the ANTs? As soon as you see them. Practise constructive thinking and climb out of the negative thinking trap.

Yoursations are not conversations

Coming to a conversation or business decision thinking you have all the facts is as pointless as going to relationship counselling on your own. When you're the only one contributing, or you are prepared to listen solely to *your* version of the facts, you are more likely to see flawed outcomes as a result. After all, you're only focusing on Number One, not taking into account all the factors and opinions surrounding you.

I call these types of conversations 'yoursations'—don't interrupt me while I am letting you hear what I'm saying.

A CONVERSATION SHOULD FEEL LIKE A *tennis rally*—BACK AND FORTH, BACK AND FORTH.

We've all been on the receiving end of a 'conversation' with someone who loves hearing the sound of their own voice. Perhaps you can be brave enough to admit that sometimes you might momentarily fall into this category as well.

It's time for those who take most of the available airtime to learn about yoursations. You can practically have them without the other person. You just can't see it because you're too busy having your point heard or telling your stories. If you're this sort of person you may often wonder why people don't listen to you. You are completely caught up in your own talking, and you don't listen.

Let's think about a conversation as a seesaw. When you are talking the most, you are at the highest point of the seesaw and the person you are talking to is down the bottom. Being bombarded by your content, your voice—being talked at. Perhaps feeling undervalued, disrespected; definitely feeling unheard. There needs to be an even tipping of the plank for a productive conversation to take place; otherwise it's a yoursation (see figure 4.3).

Figure 4.3: do you have conversations or yoursations?

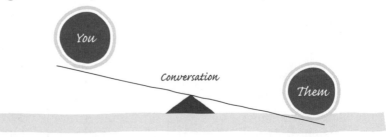

So why do we do talk *at* others so easily?

Social psychologist Gemma Cribb says the people most likely to be over-talkers are:

- people who are nervous and anxious to please the person they are talking to
- narcissists, who can't imagine anything more important than what they have to say
- people with disorders such as Asperger's, who have trouble picking up on social cues.

If these feel a little too harsh, the other reasons are typically:

- a lack of self-awareness leading to focusing on yourself too much
- a bad habit of cutting people off and talking way too much (also known as verbal diarrhoea).

Aside from these popular insights, there is another way to understand why 'yoursationalists' do this. When people don't feel safe enough in a conversation they can fall into the yoursation trap, either out of nerves or out of the need to be right and win. We examine these fight-and-flight behaviours in chapter 6.

Silence is not permission

I was working with a team to improve their internal and external brand reputation. Part of the program was to observe some of their meetings and interactions with each other and their stakeholders. I watched the director present next year's strategy to the group. He asked if there were any questions. There weren't any, and so after three seconds he moved to the implementation plan and allocated tasks and timelines to those in the room. I asked his opinion of how the meeting went. He thought it was a great success as he had an agreed action plan with no objections.

I asked the team members the same question. The consensus was that it went the way meetings usually do: an hour of being talked at, with little opportunity for contribution.

This behaviour by the team is called 'passive agreement' and it is damaging. It is sadly very common in organisations across the globe, including many of the clients I work with. People would rather avoid disagreements and conflict with others, so they agree or they say nothing.

Both parties need to take responsibility for the damage this causes. Those who lead the yoursations need to start looking out for people being silent or passively agreeing. Those who hold back from sharing their perspectives also need to be aware that this does not result in the best decisions or outcomes for the organisation, their team or themselves.

Passive agreement typically happens when people don't feel safe enough in a conversation to pipe up and share their perspective. They fear the conflict it might create, or they're afraid that they might not be right, or that their perspective might not be good enough. It could be any of these reasons, but the point it is that it doesn't contribute to the best decision-making or to building respectful relationships.

So if you want to understand how to make the best decisions, and build the respect and trust of your teams, ask them questions and then…shut the hell up! Don't be a dick. It will make a difference and you might even learn something.

The Dalai Lama tells us 'When you talk, you are only repeating what you already know. But if you listen, you may learn something new'. After all, all you have is your perspective and that's not the real truth. That's just *your* truth.

Your truth is not the 'real truth'

The project manager makes a decision to move the deadline for the project out by two more weeks. The production team will not be able to build the prototype on time as originally planned. He has gathered all the facts about why this occurred (not his opinions of the facts) and let marketing know so they can delay the launch. That's just the way it has to be. Marketing tells the project manager that they will not be able to work with the new timeframe as they are already planning three other launches in that week. He lets them know this is unsatisfactory and that his date is the priority.

How well do you think this will go?

While the project manager might have been accurate in presenting the actual facts of the situation, and not his opinion or feelings, we still have a problem. He believes that his truth, which is that his product needs to be the priority, is the 'real truth'. However, the 'real truth' is when all parties share what they know to be true. It is a combination of what *you* know and what *they* know that leads to great decision-making, better outcomes and improved relationships.

YOUR *truth* + THEIR *truth* = THE REAL *truth*

What the project manager doesn't know, because he hasn't asked, is that two of three product launches could be moved if he speaks to his colleagues. What he also doesn't know (because he chose to have a yoursation rather than a conversation) is that a couple of his team members are about to take pre-approved leave, which means his new deadline will now be a major challenge. He also doesn't know that his new launch date falls at the same time that the major competitor is rebranding, so the impact might be reduced.

If the project manager holds his ground here and demands the new timeline, then he is likely to damage the relationship with the marketing team and cause a poor outcome for the business, unnecessary pressure on everyone in the team to deliver to unreasonable timeframes, and budget blowouts. All because he decided that his truth was the 'real truth'.

When you have all the facts, all the variables and are aware of all the potential blockers you can address people's concerns, navigate the issues and allow people to feel heard. Of course, it is unlikely that everyone will be on the same page, but feeling heard and valued counts significantly.

The implications of not having all the information are that it can lead to erroneous decision-making—which can affect customers, colleagues, strategy and reputation, right along the business food chain.

The same thing happens when we tell a customer that we are changing the terms of the contract without understanding the implications for them. We need to understand their perspective, and they ours, for ideal outcomes.

EXPAND THE CONVERSATION

One of the greatest gifts you can give someone is not your advice but your attention. The goal should be to expand the conversation, not narrow it.

- Imagine you went to the doctor and he did all the tests (bloods, blood pressure, reflex) but did not ask you what your symptoms were.

- Imagine you went to a new high-end restaurant and the waiter decided to serve you the specials because they were fabulous.

- Imagine you went to a performance review and your manager told you your developmental goals for the next 12 months without your input?

Which one is most likely? We all know the answer to that.

If you want to maintain great relationships with people *and* make the best decisions for optimum outcomes then get the 'real truth', not just *your* truth. Hey, you might even learn something along the way.

I saw this post recently and think it sums it up perfectly:

> If I offered you $100 000 to jump out of a plane with no parachute would you do it? I bet you would say no. But what if I told you the plane was on the ground?

Moral of the story: know all the facts before you open your mouth.

Your cheat sheet

- It is a combination of what *you* know and what *they* know that leads to great decision-making, better outcomes and improved relationships.

- Honesty is not an excuse to verbally assassinate someone. When we speak we create an emotional wake that we should take ownership of.

- Separate the facts from your opinions and feelings. People need facts to understand exactly what is not working, or what needs improvement. They don't need your thoughts about it.

- Speculation gets in the way of remarkable conversations. Facts don't damage relationships and outcomes. They are the foundations of the discussion.

- About 95 per cent of our thoughts are essentially the same every day, and 80 per cent of those are negative. Don't accept the ANTs (Automatic Negative Thoughts); they lead to speculation and poor results.

- Have conversations, not yoursations. When you're the only one contributing, or you are prepared to listen solely to your side's version of the facts, you are more likely to see flawed outcomes as a result.

- Passive agreement is not real agreement; when people do not share their perspectives, good decision-making is impossible.

- Not having all the information leads to poor decisions that can affect customers, colleagues, strategy and reputation, right along the business food chain.

Chapter 5
Having the conversation

People know when a tough conversation is about to be had. They can smell it.

Taking time to prepare for your tough conversation or feedback session makes all the difference in preserving, and even improving, your relationships and getting the best outcomes for your team and the business. Reflecting on *what* you need to say, and *how* you need to say it, *before* you actually say it, makes all the difference. Preparation also allows you to stay focused when you are in the conversation. So let's understand what we need to reflect on.

PREPARATION IS *key*.

I am a complete believer in Susan Scott's structure for starting conversations in *Fierce Conversations*. Let's look at this as a way to structure conversations to foster strong relationships, improve outcomes and boost the performance of those around you.

1   State the issue (the purpose).

2   Provide examples.

3 Share your opinions and/or feelings.

4 Clarify what is at stake.

5 Identify your contribution.

6 Indicate your intent to resolve (but do not problem-solve).

7 Ask for their perspective.

It's a good way to start the conversation. It should only take a minute (as it's just the starter). If done correctly it can stop conversations from becoming larger or smaller than they need to be.

1. State the issue (the purpose)

Take a few minutes to recall someone that you respect in your life and the characteristics of that relationship. What makes them someone you respect? What do they say or do to earn that place?

Chances are they tell it to you straight. They don't beat around the bush. They say it as it is. After all, it's what we need to hear. Sometimes it's not what we want to hear but, as we know, not all feedback is warm and fuzzy. It's often the tough messages that have the biggest impact.

No longer should we be subscribing to what we may have been taught in the past: that we need to deliver something nice, then the tough news and then wrap it again at the end with a positive bow. It's fondly known as the shit sandwich. When this is done people either don't hear the bit in the middle, which is what you're are trying to relay; or they don't respect the fact that you don't tell it straight.

So when you are preparing to give feedback or have a tough conversation, make sure you state the purpose straight away. Get straight to the point. No more elephants in the room. What do you want to talk about? Say it and it's done. It might be 'I want to discuss your performance', or 'I want to give you feedback on the client meeting' or 'I want to discuss your impact on the team'.

Say it and then it's done and no-one needs to be a mind-reader or spend time deciphering what you are trying to say. It's harder than you think—defining what the real issue is, that is. I have seen many times where people think the issue is one thing but it is really another. So be clear on the issue, because it will anchor the feedback in the right or wrong place.

The biggest tip I can share is to make sure your issue is not an opinion or a feeling. If you lead with your opinion of the issue then you are walking into gunfire.

I can recall so many conversations where it felt like it took two years for my colleague to get to their point. I have even been unsure about what the point was and had to ask, 'So what is this really about?' If you are unsure, then I can guarantee the person you're giving feedback to will be unsure also.

When the issue is unambiguous it can be an anchor to come back to when the conversation goes off the track. You need to be clear on the issue in order to drive great outcomes.

2. Provide examples

Here is where you provide facts. Not opinions, but tangible, proven information that helps the other person understand why the feedback or conversation is taking place. If they are facts, the other person cannot deny them (unless they have a poor moral or mental compass). When you are presenting information this way it will be easier to lead conversations.

Here's an example: 'I want to talk to you about the sales report you sent to the client two days late'. Start simply, but have supporting detail up your sleeve: 'You told Steve that you would deliver the report to the client by Monday. Then on Monday the client called me to say he had not received the report. On Tuesday I asked you when you were going to complete the report and you said by the end of the day. On Wednesday at 9 am I called the client and he still had not received it. He told me that this is a concern for them and how they work with us ...'

The reason we don't go into all the detail right away is because the start of the conversation would take far longer than one minute. The reason we are trying to keep it short and sharp is to extend the courtesy of having a conversation, not a yoursation. If we can't hear the other person's side early on we only have our truth and not the 'real truth', which is a combination of what you know, and they know.

So keep the initial examples very short but have the details behind them in case you need to recall them later in the conversation.

Beware!!! If you don't have any examples I would suggest you don't have a conversation. You may have an opinion or a reaction, to a person or a situation, that you need to own. Yes, it might be *your* stuff and not theirs that needs to be addressed. But more of that in chapter 7.

3. Share your opinions and/or feelings

It's good to know that your opinions and feelings matter. If they are important to you, then they are important. This is about letting the other person know how you view the impact of what has or has not happened or been said.

I recall a colleague I worked with years ago on a project and we just weren't gelling. Some examples of what made the relationship tense include that whenever I presented ideas she would either ignore my suggestions or suggest that they needed more work before we could consider them. When she was presenting to the group she would give eye contact to everyone around the table but skip my eyes. She would not respond to my emails without a second or third prompt.

So I asked her if we could discuss our working relationship. I presented my examples and suggested that there was tension in our relationship that I would like to understand. To be honest, I was not enjoying working with her but I knew that leading the conversation with that wouldn't be helpful if I truly wanted an improved relationship — and better results, which could only come if we collaborated effectively. She told me she just didn't like me. I asked for some examples of how she came to that conclusion. I got nothing. We can't work with everyone well. I know that. I also know that some personalities just rub others up the wrong way. However, without examples your opinions and feelings have little impact and can end up damaging relationships.

Opinions have a place but they are never something that you lead feedback with. After all, they are not facts — just your truth. We also have to be very careful that our judgements aren't clouded by our 'cognitive distortions' (the way we see information and data and then recalibrate it based on our own beliefs and values).

In the earlier example, where Steve did not deliver the report to the client on time, the impact of the situation might be:

- putting the client relationship at risk
- creating concern about your team members' performance
- feeling disappointed about the lack of commitment to timelines
- feeling concerned that Steve did not let you or the client know that the deadline would not be met.

All of these are relevant but they are not what you lead with. They are your opinions and feelings and, as you can see from this example, there can be several perspectives depending on how you view things.

We need to self-check here that we are not speculating — creating and telling ourselves a story about the person. About how they are thinking or feeling or what is going on for them. Stories have no place in tough conversations and should be avoided at all costs.

4. Clarify what is at stake

What is the impact of the action or inaction of the person you are having a conversation with? What are the repercussions? What are the stakes in not improving or handling the issue better? What is at stake for the person if they do not act on the information you are giving them?

It is very important to be clear about the stakes. Often people need this to be spelt out so it is very clear for them. I find that the person giving the feedback tends to shy away from this, yet later wonders why the other person did not fully understand how serious the issue is. Being clear allows them to understand the full impact of their actions. The higher the stakes on what you are discussing, the more important this becomes. For example:

- 'If you don't improve then we will have to go down a formal performance management process and your first warning will be issued.'

- 'If we cannot change the timeframes then we will not be able to produce the units in time for the customer and we may lose them altogether.'

- 'If we don't improve our working relationship it sets a poor example for the rest of the team and we are unlikely to do our best work.'

So what is at stake? Write it down and say it. There is no other way. The stakes explain why you are having the conversation. It often creates the shift, as people might not otherwise see the 'what if' they don't change or improve.

On the other hand, if the stakes are really low then so is the impact—and in some cases the issue may be not worth mentioning. It may be you are just nipping something in the bud for the first time, or providing direction on something such as how to close a customer call with more success, or a better way to present to a client, or how to run a meeting more effectively. Sometimes it's just good old-fashioned feedback intended to help someone to become better at their job.

5. Identify your contribution

When giving feedback I often find that it takes two to tango. While what you are presenting to your colleague is important, there is often something you can own. The more we own and show our own flaws, the more likely others are to do the same.

We often come to conversations or feedback sessions hoping the other person will be open to what we are sharing. We want them to understand, own their stuff and apologise if necessary. So we need to show them that we are prepared to so the same thing. Otherwise it lacks integrity and we are not leading by example.

It might be apologising for not being as clear on expectations as you should have been, or for not offering enough support, or for presenting a strategy without their input. For some reason we really struggle with apologies, yet we expect them from others.

Apologies can make a big difference. When an apology is coated with genuine self-reflection its delivery goes a long way towards building and repairing trust and respect.

GENUINE *apologies* PROMOTE RECONCILIATION.

I'm now a lover of taking ownership, because I see what a difference it makes when giving feedback and how it can break down tension. I experienced this when a really close friend had the courage to let me know that while she valued my 'directness' it sometimes made her feel inadequate and insecure. At the same time she gave me the feedback (with relevant examples) she also said that she needed to own her own sensitivities and reactions to my style. She knew my heart was in the right place but it was just too confronting for her. It was much easier to stomach what she was saying when I felt she was owning some of the issue.

So if there is something you should own—own it! Set the tone for how you want the conversation to go. If there is nothing at all you need to own, double check yourself.

There is a line here to be careful of. In some cases there may not be anything you need to take responsibility for. And in other cases you may take too much responsibility. If the conversation is important enough for you to have, and the stakes are obvious, then be careful not to downplay its importance by owning things that you don't need to.

IF IT'S NOT YOURS, DON'T OWN IT

I was mentoring a client and we were structuring the conversation she needed to have with her business partner. Based on the evidence, she felt she was taking the lion's share of the work (opinion) and if it continued she was likely to burn out, and it could affect their relationship as she would feel resentful for doing more (stakes). She then felt she needed to apologise for taking on all the work when her partner was not around.

What the?

She just lost the impact and the point she was trying to make. If the evidence is strong enough and you don't need to own anything (aside from not mentioning the issue earlier), then don't own it.

6. Indicate your intent to resolve (but do not problem-solve)

People need to know you sincerely want to find a resolution; otherwise they will tend to feel threatened and unsafe. Your intent might be authentic, but people can't see your intent so they need to hear it. This is where you might let people know that you're keen to reach an outcome or better understand the situation.

This is not about coming up with solutions.

Why? Because without the other person's facts and explanations, how can you make the best recommendation? There is no collaboration in presenting a solution without understanding the other person's perspective.

For many people delivering feedback, there's some peace of mind in not having to come up with a solution for a problem or issue that has presented itself. They can have some ideas up their sleeve but they are discussed with the other person. Rarely should someone be presented *at*. Collaboration is about doing it together.

You may say something like:

- 'I am keen to understand your side of the story'
- 'I just want to work out the best way to move forward'
- 'I just want to support you to be even better'.

State your intent to come to a resolution, and then discuss the potential solutions *after* you understand the other person's side.

7. Ask for their perspective

Finally, the way to end any feedback conversation is by showing your genuine interest in understanding the other person's perspective. If you don't, you will only have your truth, not the real truth.

It is a combination of what *you* know and what *they* know that leads to great decision-making, remarkable outcomes and stronger relationships. Not having all the information (or discounting some of it) leads to poor decision-making that can affect your customers, colleagues, strategy and reputation, right along the business food chain.

Finishing the conversation with something along the lines of: 'What are your thoughts?' or 'What's your perspective?' or 'How does this sit with you?' is a simple way to complete the process.

And then be prepared to listen. Really listen. And receive the feedback as gracefully as you would like the other person to.

Too many conversations finish with a solution or a 'Here's my opinion, full-stop' mentality. Of course this is not going to promote trust and respect. It's just a command-and-control strategy that was common in the 1940s.

* * *

Prepare your feedback conversation using this format and practise it out loud. If it's longer than a minute, chances are you have too much in there. Give the other person time to respond quickly so that it feels like a shared discussion, and watch the conversation and relationships flow.

Now it's your turn. Use this structure to plan out a conversation you need to have.

1 State the issue (the purpose).

2 Provide examples.

3 Share your opinions and/or feelings.

4 Clarify what is at stake.

5 Identify your contribution.

6 Indicate your intent to resolve (but do not problem-solve).

7 Ask for their perspective.

The ideal method

It's common in the contemporary workplace for people to work from different locations. Whether it is working from home, or working in different states and countries, technology enables it. But with this flexibility comes the challenge of communication and collaboration. Too often, 'my team is not next to me' becomes the excuse to not have conversations that need to be had.

If you learn and practise the art of having remarkable conversations then maintaining a high-performing team is well and truly possible. The leader and the team just need to be committed to the art, even if we don't have the luxury of working face-to-face. It can be that simple.

Table 5.1 details the outcomes you are likely to reach depending on the medium you use to deliver feedback. You will see that anything less than a phone call is an ineffective and often damaging way of giving feedback.

Table 5.1: feedback methods and their outcomes

Method	Outcome
Face-to-face	Ideal
Face-to-face (tech-assisted)	Near 100% positive
Phone	Highly likely to be positive
Email	Highly unlikely to be positive
Text	Dangerous
Snapchat or Facebook	Epic fail

The more face-to-face conversations you have the greater your chance of reaching a positive outcome. Unfortunately, many people hide behind emails as a way of delivering tough information. Email has its uses but when it comes to having the tough conversations, which may be emotional and have considerable implications for one or both parties, email is not the way.

Having a tough conversation successfully by email is as likely as successfully putting together an IKEA wardrobe without the instructions. It could happen, but it would be a fluke. There is a furphy out there that it softens the blow and takes the emotion out of the feedback. It doesn't. Why? People can easily misread your tone and your intent, and the opportunity for interaction is limited.

The right place at the right time

Giving feedback and having the tough conversations as soon as you see the issue is a display of remarkable leadership. Not waiting until an issue happens over and over again is a sign of leadership excellence. Most feedback conversations become bigger than they need to be because issues aren't nipped in the bud as soon as they arise. Remarkable leaders are those that regularly hold others to account.

As discussed in chapter 2, failing to have tough conversations and nip problems in the bud is costly: ignoring an issue could mean the difference between dealing with a spot fire and battling a raging bushfire. The longer we leave it, the greater the costs to the business and ourselves.

I was working through an issue with a client recently, regarding a significant performance conversation with one of his store managers. The store manager was making offensive comments about his staff, his style was viewed as aggressive and intimidating, and he would often get angry in front of customers. The store found it hard to retain good people; sales were not improving; a mental health claim regarding bullying had been made; and customers would leave when they witnessed his outbursts. When I asked how long this had been going on he told me, 'Oh, at least 12 months'. Unfortunately this is not an unusual scenario.

If you let issues occur over and over again, you have a few problems:

- It becomes harder (mainly for you) to have the conversation, as you have let it fester in your mind for so long. Emotions are likely to be strong in this scenario, too, as your frustration may build or your avoidance and awkwardness about confronting the issue rises.

- The incident, as it has been repeating itself, has now affected other people and parts of the business. The person's behaviours and/or words may have affected other people, systems, processes and customers, and may even have led to poor decisions being made on behalf of the business. You now have a bigger mess to clean up than if you'd addressed it up-front.

- You have missed the opportunity to support the individual's growth and development. Training is important, but feedback about how to become a better version of yourself is essential. As a leader or valued colleague you have the opportunity to give someone the 'gift' of your feedback. They then have the opportunity to improve and grow and develop.

- Your relationship with the person may now be at risk. While the individual ultimately needs to take responsibility for their own actions or inactions, they can feel justified in being disappointed that you were not up-front and honest with them when it was an issue at the start. Respect and trust may be damaged and will need to be repaired.

Don't forget, the people around you that you really respect are those who are honest with you. They have the courage to have the tough conversations and say it as it is. This is just as true in the workplace as it is in your personal life.

So what we know is that:

- if you do nothing, nothing will change
- it is highly likely that the action will repeat itself or get worse
- it costs the organisation *and* the individual avoiding the issue
- a remarkable conversation is likely to influence change.

Location, location

The formula for bringing about outstanding outcomes is to give feedback at the right time, in the right way, in the right place. We have learned the power of communicating feedback as soon as we see a problem arise. The other factor we need to consider is where we choose to give the feedback.

Working in an open-plan space is common nowadays. Even if we are committed to the 'nipping it in the bud' concept, we need to be sensitive to privacy considerations. People can feel exposed if they are given feedback in front of their colleagues. I do see this more often than I would like to.

Just last year I was walking through a client's office, all open-plan. I heard what appeared to be a supervisor letting their colleague know that if they were late to work one more time then they would receive a formal warning. You could have cut the air with a knife. There were no questions asked about the reason for being late — the employee was being spoken *at*, the tone of the supervisor was aggressive and her voice was loud enough that everyone around them heard.

If someone feels exposed in front of others they are likely to feel vulnerable, shamed and disrespected. We need to create a safe place where people can be honest and reflect and share appropriately. Stalling in the moment, and asking to grab a room or have a coffee soon after, is best practice in these circumstances.

Conversations or feedback moments can arise at any time, in one-on-one meetings, in team meetings, in a conversation in the kitchen, in a taxi back from a meeting. Anytime and anywhere. But just because we want to have the conversation now does not mean it will lead to the best outcome.

TIMING + *method* + LOCATION = *great* OUTCOMES AND RELATIONSHIPS

We don't always have the luxury of controlling the timing of tough conversations. Ideally we have time to prepare, but many of them are unplanned or sprung on us with little time, or no time, for preparation. (Luckily there are many tools and techniques for facilitating a remarkable conversation, irrespective of who is driving it.) In one-on-one situations the timing is *now*, but there are times when immediate action might not appropriate.

On the other hand, if the feedback is positive then sharing it in front of others may be okay. We just need to consider whether the person will receive it well in front of others. Some people are highly embarrassed being singled out, even when it's good news.

Giving positive feedback in front of others can certainly backfire. I once worked with a leader who would regularly highlight the outstanding performance of one of his team members in team meetings and around the office. You would think this would be a good thing, right?! It was a problem because the leader gave this person positive feedback, and no-one else. The team felt that the favouritism was clear, and it was demotivating. They were not recognised for the contributions they made.

We just need to be sensitive about the location we choose, that's all.

Conflict is good

Once you build up enough courage to have the tough conversations, the next big block that I often see is a poor relationship with conflict. Many people either aren't comfortable with conflict, or create way too much tension for the conflict to be productive.

If we agreed all the time we would never have the gift of shared thinking, or coming up with the best way of doing and seeing things, or building highly creative and innovative workplaces. While conflict can result from clashing principles, it can also push boundaries and challenge the status quo. Our negative attitude to conflict tends to cloud our ability to deal with it. Embracing it can be counterintuitive to what we know.

Sporting teams are okay with conflict. There would not be a match without it. There are those who avoid conflict and those who manage it poorly. Just think of Steve Jobs, who was voted out of any active leadership role by his own board at Apple. His poor collaboration skills prevented him from building great relationships and making the best business decisions. He failed to do the thinking and decision-making *with* his people. He was comfortable with conflict; while he is certainly known for his genius, his legacy is also his command-and-control style.

Margaret Heffernan was educated at Cambridge University and is the author of four books. She speaks to corporations, associations, universities and education conferences about continuous innovation, managing high-achieving talent and about the role of leaders in serving the talent they hire. She tells us that openness alone cannot drive change. Openness isn't the end. It's the beginning. Nor does being right drive change.

In her TED talk 'Dare to Disagree', Margaret Heffernan recommends 'We need to find "thinking partners" who are not echo chambers of our own thinking'. Some think that surrounding themselves with a group of people who agree with their thinking is a good thing — good because they can move forward quickly and get things done. They believe that less conflict + less drama = happy workplace.

People who want to drive innovation and improvement and become a better version of themselves and their workplaces need to think differently. We need to push each other and become comfortable with thinking partners that allow conflict.

If you see conflict as healthy thinking it allows people to speak up, bring new ideas to the table and have tough conversations more regularly.

So why do we dislike conflict?

- *We are not used to it.* Healthy conflict is not often part of our upbringing, workplaces, social circles or culture. I remember going to relationship counselling with my partner at the time, when I was in my early thirties. The counsellor asked us how our parents resolved arguments. My parents didn't mind a good old verbal swinging match every now and then, but I could not recall seeing any apologies or conversations to clear them up. They just got on with it after an argument — as far as I could see. (Of course, that was not really the case, but that was my observation growing up. Except for the time that Mum did not talk to Dad for 21 days in a row. That was a doozy.)

My partner grew up in a home where conflict was avoided, so arguments and tension were not 'normal'. We had to learn that conflict was okay and resolution was essential. Key learnings for both of us. Another example is when you started your first job. Your confidence is not that high but your passion and motivation is (well, at least for most of us). You observe all the experienced achievers in the room and decide you would rather say nothing than look stupid. So you avoid offering a suggestion or an opinion if it differs from what they are saying. In other words, you avoid. This avoidance then often continues throughout your career, even as you gain more experience and runs on the board.

- *We take different opinions personally.* Conflict may challenge our ego, our sense of self, and that feeling of not being good enough. When you come up with an idea or suggestion that you believe is great, how do you feel when someone else shoots it down or comes up with something they think is better? I'll be honest. I can find that challenging. I often feel like they are rejecting me personally, not just my idea. Sometimes it can be hard to separate the idea from the person, but it is necessary.

- *It represents a loss.* It's all about someone winning and someone losing. Having to know it all and have all the answers and ideas is a place where some people live. So when conflict occurs and perspectives are being challenged, it is uncomfortable. This often leads to feelings of loss, resentment, anger, and hostility. Ever travelled with someone and had a fight about which direction to take, when looking at a map? You say left, he says right. Then all of a sudden it's on. Why does one person have to be right? Why can't we discuss it and share our thinking?

Managing your relationship to conflict

I find the well-known and widely used Thomas-Kilmann conflict model (see figure 5.1) a good way for people to understand where they fit in their relationship to conflict. It plots those who have concern for others on the vertical axis and those with concern for self on the horizontal.

Figure 5.1: Thomas-Kilmann conflict model

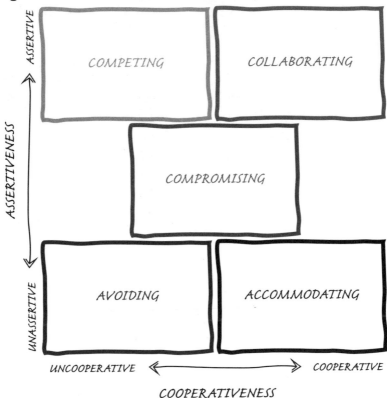

You would think that being concerned about others' welfare, ideas, opinions and feelings would be a good thing, right? Generally it is. However, when it compromises your own sense of self-worth, it becomes unhelpful.

You will see that people whose concern for self *and* others is low fall into the Avoiding space. Their desire to resolve things is not motivated by what others think or by what they think of themselves, so they stay trapped in doing nothing about it. They lack assertiveness and they lack cooperation. Avoidance can also look like passive agreement (where a person says yes but has no intention of delivering, or they put off the deadline, or they sidestep the issue). It is a very unhealthy holding pattern where things do not get done.

People who have a greater concern for others but don't value their own contribution or self as much tend to fall into the Accommodating space. They say yes to whatever the other person or other group wants. They believe that their opinion does not matter as much as others'. These people are controlled by others. They lack assertiveness yet are cooperative. They can be easily coerced or manipulated into a way of thinking that is not their own.

People who value their own contribution more than they value the contribution of others are highly assertive and lacking in collaboration. They are known as Competing. They need to win, get their idea through and be right, at all costs. They are not great at listening or taking other ideas on board.

Then we have the Collaborators, who have a healthier mix of concern for self and concern for others. They are appropriately assertive *and* open to others' perspectives. They look for the win–win, where both parties can walk away feeling satisfied. They will dig to find a solution that suits everyone. They are comfortable exploring different options and discussing different points of view. They can get stuck if both parties are not satisfied.

In the middle of the conflict model is Compromising. Sitting between Competing and Accommodating, these people give up more than they compete—but less often than those in Accommodating. They address the issues more than the Avoiders but don't explore issues as much as the Collaborators. They possess a blend of concern for self and concern for others, but are also prepared to back down if there is a decision stalemate, or to meet halfway to move forward.

Where do you sit in the model? How does your relationship to control affect your ability to communicate and collaborate with your friends and colleagues?

Of course, most people want to know what the ideal place is. The answer is: it depends. In some situations you may be required to be more of one than another. For example, if you are a barrister in a court of law then you will err on the Competing side, as you need to win for your client—no matter the cost. If you are negotiating a new contract with a client it might be that Collaborating or Compromising is the ideal. You need to find the right blend for your situation. I suggest that Avoiding should be a no-go zone at all times. There is nothing to come or change from it.

Margaret Heffernan and Linda Adams suggest there are three steps to improving our attitude to conflict and seeing it in a positive light.

1 *Reframe your attitude to conflict.* If we decide conflict is bad, how will this help us? If we are open to conflict being healthy then the way we step into situations and conversations will shift significantly. I work with many people and organisations where passive agreement has become the norm. Agreeing to things even when we don't, because we don't think the conflict will be productive, has the opposite effect. It leads to a place where no-one discusses the very issues they should be discussing, so poor performance, client relationships, leadership, strategic decisions keep occurring. We think that having the conflict is pointless. Well, guess what? If you think that way, you're probably right—it won't. You need to think differently to drive change for the better.

2 *Have the courage and drive to learn.* Many years ago I bought a pair of $500 rollerblades. It was an initiative that we girls thought was a good idea at the time. We all lived by the beach and wanted to scoot up and down the footpaths looking like we were out of a scene from *Xanadu.* We wanted to look the goods and get fit at the same time. We got out the first day for 30 minutes. Our calves

were hurting and we kept falling over. We were next to a pub so we thought we'd pop in for 'one'. We have never rollerbladed since. I ended up selling my rollerblades on eBay for $70. We simply weren't willing to push ourselves to develop the talent and skills (and courage) to become better.

3   *Develop the skills to communicate well.* I could not agree more that this is crucial! You might have the right attitude and have developed the courage to communicate. But if you do a poor job of handling conflict respectfully then it's back to square one. There is, after all, a difference between productive conflict and just plain arguing.

Your body language has a profound effect … on you!

You may have heard the saying, 'It's not what you say, but how you say it that makes the biggest difference' or 'People don't remember what you said but they remember how you made them feel'. While these sayings ring true, there is also another component — body language. Body language affects how others see us. Looking confident in our stance, maintaining eye contact, and being open to information with our arms unfolded is important. It makes an impression, and people make decisions based on what they see and how it makes them feel rather than on the content of what you're saying. But body language may also change how we see *ourselves*.

We are now learning that the way we hold ourselves has a profound impact on the way we feel about ourselves.

Amy Cuddy, an associate professor at Harvard Business School, has done some remarkably compelling research on the impact of our body language on *ourselves*. Body language includes everything from eye contact (direct, averting, on and off), body positioning (slouching, sitting up straight, standing versus sitting, where you place your hands), proximity of the other person (close or far away, higher or lower) and listening (actively or passively).

OUR NON-VERBAL *cues* GOVERN HOW WE *feel* ABOUT OURSELVES.

We know our minds change our behaviours. Is it also possible for our bodies to change our minds and then in turn our behaviours? Cuddy says it is.

When powerful leaders (men and women) take charge they have high levels of testosterone and secrete low levels of cortisol (stress hormone). Cuddy says that powerful poses can really change the way you feel about yourself. Keep this in mind when you are lacking confidence or scared stiff before a speaking engagement, job interview, important pitch, difficult meeting or, of course, one of those tough conversations.

Tiny tweaks can lead to big changes. It's about configuring your brain to cope in those situations by using your physical demeanour to then influence your mind and therefore your behaviours. It's good to know that:

- our bodies change our minds
- our minds change our behaviours
- our behaviours change our outcomes.

So, try a power pose! Wonder Woman or Superman. Hold yourself with grace and authority like President Obama or Beyoncé.

Before your next conversation, find a space and expand. Make yourself big for at least two minutes and then observe how this changes the way you feel and helps to steady your nerves. This exercise will lead to a noticeable change in the way others interact with you as well.

Your Cheat Sheet

- Preparing for the tough conversations preserves relationships and improves outcomes. Follow these simple guidelines:

  1 State the issue (the purpose).

  2 Provide examples.

  3 Share your opinions and/or feelings.

  4 Clarify what is at stake.

  5 Identify your contribution.

  6 Indicate your intent to resolve (but do not problem-solve).

  7 Ask for their perspective.

- Choose the delivery method wisely—and the time and place.

- Conflict can be a good thing when it comes to making great decisions.

- If we stay comfortable with people who always think like we do they will become 'echo chambers' and this does not encourage new thinking and ideas.

- Our relationship to conflict hinges upon how we communicate and collaborate with those around us.

- When we can reframe the way we view conflict then we learn to manage ourselves well in difficult interactions.

- Body language not only dictates other people's perceptions of us, it also affects the way we feel about ourselves.

- If we use our physicality in a positive and assertive way when in challenging conversations, it can help our view of ourselves and build confidence.

Chapter 6
IT'S ALL ABOUT SAFETY

Maintaining 'safety' in a conversation is the difference between an outcome and an outbreak. It's when both parties feel 'safe enough' to be honest with each other that you reach the best outcomes and preserve great working relationships. I first became inspired by this idea after reading about the importance of maintaining the 'safe zone' in VitalSmarts' *Crucial Conversations*. I have since then added to their thinking.

Management expert and author Ken Blanchard says that 'real communication happens when people feel safe'. This is not a 'warm and fuzzy' space. It's about having a constructive conversation that leads to an outcome.

When things go wrong in a conversation we assume the content is the problem, so we water it down, sugar-coat it or avoid it altogether in the hope that the other person will do the heavy lifting and see the truth hidden underneath. Or we do the opposite: we have a strong reaction and go into battle with our 'opponent' in an effort to be seen as right.

No wonder the outcomes we are looking for (changed behaviour, better performance, improved attitudes) don't happen—we let our emotional reactions become the priority rather than the content or purpose of the conversation.

But here's the good news. As long as your intent is good and you learn how to make it safe for others, you can give feedback and have tough conversations with almost anyone about almost anything. Many people do not believe there can be a marriage between being candid and being kind. But there can be.

So the challenge, then, is to create a safe zone where all parties feel safe enough to discuss the real issues and do not have to deal with their emotional reactions and repercussions.

Are you a fighter or a flighter?

Why do conversations go south so quickly, or end up being unproductive because the real issues are not discussed?

When we don't feel safe in a situation or conversation we have a stress reaction. This happens when our emotional or physical safety is challenged. In the case of our emotional safety, it may be that our ego is being crushed, our sense of self is being challenged, or that we are not feeling valued or heard. Threats to our physical safety are easier to notice. When we feel that we may be physically harmed it is clear when fear sets in, whether it is because someone is holding our arm too tightly or showing a clenched fist or, in extreme cases, threatening violence.

When we have these stress reactions our bodies go into a fight-or-flight response, or both. So why does this happen?

We all have stress reactions. We have been aware of them since prehistoric times. They kicked in to support our need to protect ourselves and our families when the threat of sabre-toothed tiger attack was imminent and we needed to either stay and fight, or take flight and run. The term 'fight or flight' was originally coined by Harvard physiologist Walter Cannon in 1915.

Figure 6.1 shows what happens to us when we perceive a threat to our emotional or physical safety.

Figure 6.1: fight or flight

Fight-or-flight
reaction

Perceived
threat

Physical and
psychological
response

Acute stress

Reduced
cortisol
and blood flow

Your brain perceives a threat, physical or emotional. The threat might not be real, but it is your *perception* of the threat that causes the reaction. (For example: someone gives you feedback about your leadership style and they are coming from an authentic place of wanting to help you become even better. You don't hear the message as it is intended; you feel it is a personal attack and perceive it as an emotional threat.)

You then have a physical and psychological response, which may include your heart beating faster, your palms getting sweaty, your face going pale and your breathing becoming faster. You may also experience chest pains, a dry mouth, tense muscles or rapid breathing. The nervous system automatically puts the body on alert, and with all of this going on it's no wonder it's difficult to concentrate on the content of a conversation.

This stress response then reduces blood flow to the brain. The blood automatically diverts to major muscles, such as arms and legs, to prepare your body to protect itself. At the same time, the adrenal cortex automatically releases stress hormones. You know how you walk away from a challenging conversation and then think of a hundred things you could have said but they were a million miles away from your brain at the time? This is why that happens. You are no longer clearly hearing what people are saying, because you are not thinking clearly. The blood has rushed from your brain and into your major muscles and vital organs.

Can you recall the last time you felt like you lost control of your ability to stay in the conversation, whether you went quiet or went on the attack? Well, that's because your brain got hijacked and went into acute stress. The challenge is learning to slow the response to a perceived threat, and choosing not to react poorly to it. Feeling unsafe is not something we can control easily, but our responses can be controlled.

Finally, your fight-or-flight reaction kicks in. The important thing to take away is that the fight-or-flight response is automatic. We all have it. The key here is to notice the stress reactions of fight-or-flight behaviours, in others and ourselves, so you can help restore safety in the conversation. It allows you to then move forward and reach an outcome or resolution.

What to look for when the FIGHT response has been triggered

Hard-core fighters are ticking time bombs if not managed well. But even mild fight behaviours can leave a wake of damaged relationships and poor business outcomes. The intent of a fighter is typically about force: forcing their opinion, their outcome or their tactic on someone else. They use strategies that attempt to convince, control or compel others to comply with their point of view.

Following are some typical fight behaviours:

- *Causing harm.* The person threatens another's character, job or physicality. This is about intentionally causing someone harm: it's moved on from just trying to win, to making it personal. This can include emotional outbursts such as 'I'll take you off this project if you say that again', or 'You are not able to do this because you are a woman'.

- *Passive aggressive.* The person indirectly expresses hostility through behaviours like procrastination, stubbornness, or a deliberate or repeated failure to accomplish requested tasks.

- *Dominating.* The person tries to steer the conversation, hijack the agenda, cut others off and constantly interrupt. Lecturing is a form of dominating. They may suggest that everyone is aware of the problem to try and coerce others to their point of view. 'Yoursationalists' tend to feel quite comfortable in this space, pushing their opinions and ideas on others.

- *Intimidating.* The person intentionally makes another feel insignificant, insecure and scared. They may do it with words ('Look at you, you little junior', or 'I would be very careful about what you say, young man'); or with their physicality (standing over someone, sitting over them, leaning in close to their face, tapping or pushing them, or puffing out their chest). It's all about having the upper hand and making it very clear that they are above another.

- *Belittling.* The person boxes-in and/or insults others so they can belittle them and win the argument. Fighters may label people as liars, failures, bad decision-makers, or too sensitive or uneducated.

What to look for when the FLIGHT response has been triggered

Peter Drucker put it well when he said 'the most important thing in communication is hearing what isn't being said'. Flighters tend to hold back information when they don't feel safe. It's often done as a way of avoiding potential problems or conflicts. They tend to avoid issues, content and people. They may even downplay a situation in the hope that the issue or person will go away.

Following are some typical flight behaviours:

- *Disguising.* The person hides. They might respond with humour or sarcasm, or minimise the problem by repeatedly denying anything is wrong. The 'I'm fine' response goes here. They try to persuade people that nothing is a problem.

- *Deflecting.* The person retreats and does not engage in the conversation or is minimal in their responses, at best. Behaviours include going silent, giving no eye contact, and checking their phone. Their answers and contributions are very short, and it is clear they do not want to be in the conversation. They want to run, and sometimes they do.

- *Passive agreement.* The person agrees to things as a way of avoiding conflict. This can be a difficult one to diagnose, and is incredibly frustrating. They say yes to things yet have no intention to deliver. They say they agree with ideas when they actually don't. They say all the right things but their actions do not reflect their words.

- *Evading.* The person evades the purpose of the conversation. You may see them changing the subject, steering away from sensitive subjects and avoiding answers. It is very frustrating for the receiver. Politicians are especially impressive at this. (However, for politicians it may be more about a tactic than it is about feeling unsafe.)

AVOIDERS ARE LIKE *turtles* THAT RETREAT INTO THEIR SHELLS. THEY CAN HIDE BUT IT DOESN'T HELP THE *situation*, THE DECISIONS OR THEIR RELATIONSHIPS.

An organisational culture of flighters is often as unhealthy as a group of fighters. Things don't get done and resentment and frustration builds.

Looking in the mirror

We have learned that we all have fight-or-flight responses when we are stressed, when our emotional or physical safety is threatened. It makes sense that the more stress you have in your life the more likely you are to fall into fight-or-flight mode as you have little reserves to self-manage. It's a natural human response. We can even move from fight to flight in one conversation.

Many years ago I met with a senior leader to discuss the strategy for the business for the next year. The previous 12 months had not been great; this meeting was pivotal, as I had learned a lot from the previous 12 months, both from a leadership and a strategic perspective. We had spent considerable time discussing the learnings in past meetings. For this meeting, I had put considerable time and thinking into my strategy. I'd also done my competitor analysis, researched what the market was looking for and had the budgets prepared. I was looking forward to presenting my ideas and workshopping what a cracking next 12 months might look like. But alas! that was not how we spent the time. Within five minutes the leader had taken over the meeting as an opportunity to rehash the things that had not gone well. It was out of nowhere and he was going red in the face, talking nonstop and often repeating information.

I apologised for interrupting (after 20 minutes of nonstop lecturing) and asked for some examples of the issues he was raising. I was told not to interrupt and to trust the information.

So what did I do? I took a deep breath to try and calm my nervous system. My self-talk kept saying 'just let it go, let him run out of steam', my eyes dropped, my palms went sweaty. I breathed and self-talked myself silly. I told myself there was some 'gold' to find in this yoursation, so to just go searching. This went on for 40 minutes. After he finished I was then flicked my strategy paper and told to present it. I was in no place to present anything.

Then all of a sudden my flight turned into fight. I stood up, put my hands on the table and, being highly emotional, I raised my voice and said something along the lines of 'I beg your pardon? You want me to present my strategy after that?' Then I felt the tears welling up. I said 'Give me five minutes to sort myself out and we will continue'. I headed for the bathroom, because I knew better than to discuss anything when I wanted to attack. The point is: you can flight *and* fight in the one conversation.

Think about a relationship at work (or at home) that challenges you. What stress responses do you typically show when in situations with this person? What behaviours do you show? What does this tell you about how you self-manage in the moment? Have a look at the typical behaviours of fighters and flighters. What tends to be your default reaction? Is there one you have to self-manage quite often?

BEING LED BY YOUR FIGHT-OR-FLIGHT *response* IS BEING A DICK. MANAGING AND SELF-REGULATING IS *remarkable*.

We need to become vigilant monitors not only of others' safety in a conversation, but also of our own. After all, it takes two to tango.

Later in this chapter I highlight specific strategies you can use to restore safety in a conversation or situation when the fight-or-flight response has been triggered. There are, though, two key components that need to be present in order to set up an environment that is safe for both parties.

1 Respect must be present.
2 There must be agreement on content.

These are not new concepts for people trying to master the art of conversation in the workplace, in relationships or even with children. Let's look at what they mean.

No respect = no point

If respect does not exist in the relationship, giving feedback or having a tough conversation will be very difficult. Your message is likely to fall on deaf ears. As noted by Kerry Patterson, Joseph Grenny, Ron McMillan and Al Switzler in *Crucial Conversations*, 'Respect is like air — you don't really notice it until it's not there. And then it's all you can think about'.

You have to add to the respect bank if you want to build lasting relationships and get things done. This means behaving in a way that is respectful to the other person.

My second boss after university was a man named Paul Jury. He taught me many great lessons about leadership and cultivating great relationships. The first one I ever learned from him was on my first day at work, in the first five minutes. As soon as I arrived, I was greeted at reception. Paul said, 'Georgia meet Helene and Jodie [the ladies on reception]. These are two of the most important people in this organisation.' The second introduction was with Eugene, the catering manager.

Being a bright-eyed, bushy-tailed junior, I had thought the very senior people were the most important. Yet I needed reception to squeeze in last-minute bookings, give me feedback on how people came across before I met them, and to know everyone in the office that I needed to know — reception knew it all. The same went for catering. I was big on having breakfasts and luncheons for clients, and who did I need onside? Yes, I needed Eugene.

The leadership team was still very important. What I learned early on, though, was that everyone matters. Everyone is important and everyone deserves to be treated with respect. Author and leadership expert Simon Sinek got it right when he said, 'If you want to be a great leader, remember to treat all people with respect at all times. For one, you never know when you'll need their help. And two, because it's a sign you respect people, which all great leaders do'.

Recall someone in your life that you don't really rate. In fact, someone you just don't respect. (Unfortunately it's usually easier to think of someone like that than someone you truly trust.) Got them in your mind? Now imagine them giving you feedback on your performance, or your style, or your character, or the way you come across to others. What's the first thing you are likely to do when they are talking to you?

Your self-talk will sound something like, 'Are you kidding me? *This* coming from *you*?' You are likely to have a fight-or-flight reaction and want to either attack or avoid. Whatever your reaction, you are highly unlikely to receive the information well. So that's what it's like to be on the receiving end of feedback from someone you don't respect. It's much the same feeling getting feedback from someone you think doesn't respect *you* — something to keep in mind when you're having a tough conversation.

I often get asked, how do you respect someone who doesn't deserve it, though? This is a tough one. If you're going to get an outcome, a resolution or make the best decision there is little way around it. So find something that you can respect about that person and hang on to it tight. It could be as simple as respecting the fact they have a job to do, or that they are your colleague. For me, it is about extending as much grace to them as I would like them to extend to me. It doesn't mean I like them. It's a bit like 'being the change you seek' that Gandhi talked about. It's about respecting the other person's humanity. In chapter 9 we cover some strategies to help get out of the negative thinking trap.

For now, just know that the minute people smell your disrespect it is unlikely they will feel safe, and unlikely you will get a constructive outcome from the conversation.

No agreement = no point

If you're not talking about the same thing you might as well not be talking at all. Not agreeing on the topic you are discussing is like playing darts with a blindfold on. The odds of being successful are really low, and it's dangerous.

Things become very difficult to discuss when there are competing agendas. There's actually *no* real discussion when there are competing agendas; you may as well be using a command-and-control strategy. ('You listen to my feedback and my feedback alone', 'You are not able to contribute your side of the story or convey the facts that are relevant', 'I tell and you listen'.) We all know how that works out. It might get you what you want in the short term, but in the long term there is little trust and respect and people will not feel safe enough to be honest with you. This could be the downfall of your leadership (and, in the worst case, your business).

Our government in Question Time is a great example of how pointless it is to have competing agendas. The parties are not prepared to discuss the others' points of view, so it's no surprise that they can't agree or reach outcomes. They are merely presenting their views in the hope of winning the argument, and this allows no time for true discussion. It's a need-to-win situation.

What I am suggesting here is that instead of having competing agendas, why not agree to discuss both? After all, the real truth is a combination of your truth plus theirs. In order to understand the real issue you need to see both perspectives. Then both parties will feel heard and you are more likely to reach the best outcome.

An example that might highlight the concept of mutual agendas is a conversation in which you're telling a team member that their performance is not up to scratch (your purpose), and they're needing you to be much clearer on expectations up front (their purpose). Or a meeting with a client who wants to discuss the poor service they are receiving (their purpose) while you want to share how difficult they are to get a hold of and how this slows decision-making (your purpose).

Can you see how important each person's agenda is to the content of the conversation?

Coming to meetings or conversations with a definitive point of view of what needs to happen, or change, or improve, is old style. That's called telling. For meetings and conversations to be successful we need the focus to be on showing others what we need, *and* asking them how this could or could not happen. Yes, there will be times when leaders need to pull rank if agreement is impossible. Assuming we are not being asked to do anything unethical or immoral, there are times when we need to go with it. But if someone doesn't feel heard they are less likely to feel safe enough to discuss all the implications and perspectives that may be relevant.

Unless you are prepared to discuss both perspectives an ideal outcome will not be reached. Nor will respect be maintained if one person is saying, 'My agenda is more important than what you have to say'.

Ensure you have agreement on the topic you need to discuss so everyone feels safe enough to have a constructive conversation.

Techniques to restore safety

We now know that when people don't feel safe they are not likely to hear what you are saying, and the opportunity to reach a constructive outcome or resolution is less likely. So when we recognise that this is occurring, the next step is to put in place some techniques to restore safety. In my 20 years of leading and training leaders I have found these seven techniques to be the most effective tools.

1. Apologise, when appropriate

Apologies matter. Especially when you or others have clearly violated respect. One of the most commonly held degrees is from Foot in Mouth University. But what is less common is the art of making an authentic apology. Apologies are worth more than gold.

When an apology is coated in authentic self-reflection it goes a long way towards building trust and respect. I mean honest self-reflection, where you own your stuff and are open about your mistake or contribution. These apologies demonstrate empathy, promote reconciliation and act as a proactive step forward in re-establishing the relationship. They are needed when you or others have clearly violated the respect of an individual or a group.

Researchers Lewicki and Tomlinson from the Ohio State University Fisher College of Business have found that 'people who are wronged in a business transaction may be more likely to say they would reconcile if the offender offers a sincere apology rather than just making an attempt to placate them'. This is particularly the case if the offender takes personal blame for the misdeed rather than blaming outside forces.

Genuine apologies also deliver positive outcomes in lawsuits, according to Dr Jennifer Robbennolt, a professor of law and psychology at the University of Illinois. She says, 'Conventional wisdom has been to avoid apologies because they amount to an admission of guilt that can be damaging to defendants in court. But the studies suggest apologies can actually play a positive role in settling legal cases'.

I'm not talking about the apologies that some people hand out like pamphlets. We all know someone who is a serial apologiser. There are also those people who apologise as a way of avoiding conflict. I can hear my 12-year-old son now after he 'taps' his sister hard on the back, then says 'sorry, sorry, sorry, sorry, sorry'.

JUST SAY *sorry*. AND MEAN IT! IT'S ONE OF THE BIGGEST *diffusers* AVAILABLE.

So why do we find apologising so hard?

Apologies are uncomfortable for most people because they make us vulnerable, and they may be used against us. If we admit we blew it then that could be thrown back in our face later. Or worse, the receiver might reject our apology because they may not be ready to acknowledge or receive it, and then where does that leave us? With serious egg on our face. It is this uncertainty that gives the apology such power and impact. Putting yourself out there and owning your stuff is a courageous thing to do.

John Kador, author of *Effective Apology*, defines an apology as the 'willingness to value the relationship more than the need to be right'. It can be excruciating to face ourselves (and others) when we have offended or hurt them. Kador says we are afraid to apologise because we don't want to say too much (or not enough) and make things worse. And for those of you who need to win the discussion, and find the very thought of an apology enough to give you a hernia, then consider that an apology is a good way to have the last word (she says, tongue in cheek).

The perception of apology has moved from a sign of weakness to a sign of strength. An apology is now a sign of great leadership as leaders model accountability, transparency and humility.

It's not cost-free but it's cheaper than what it reflects—which is denial and movement away from trust and respect. Not apologising is for dicks. Remarkable people offer apologies and mean them.

2. Make your comments about do and don'ts

This is about clarifying the goal and showing your intent. It is about putting both of you on the same map. Some people become very nervous about where the conversation is heading and this is a good way of clarifying your intent (which they have no idea about until you spell it out).

Using do and don't comments also helps the conversation stay on track. How many times have you gone to discuss one topic and then found yourself on the defensive because it has swung over to you or to someone or something else? You end up wondering how it happened and how you can get things back on track. This technique is your magic ticket.

Some examples of this technique include:

- 'I'm certainly not intending to make this difficult for you. What I would like to do is ensure that we make the right assessment.'

- 'What I don't want to do is lose you in my team. What I do want to do is discuss your performance.'
- 'I don't want you to feel unheard. I do need to meet a deadline though.'
- 'I don't want you to feel concerned. I just want to understand what happened.'

This is an amazing technique and the feedback I receive from participants after they put it into practice is outstanding.

3. Gain agreement

We have learned that there can be more than one purpose in a discussion. If one person does not believe the other person is prepared to discuss their point of view then they are unlikely to feel safe. This is about discussing both agendas.

If you feel that the point is getting lost, then it might be as simple as restating the purpose of the discussion. Sometimes people can get lost in the emotional stuff, and reframing the conversation is a helpful kick back into the safe zone.

This is why it's so important to get the purpose of the conversation right. If you are not centred on the right purpose you can get lost very easily. At one of my workshops recently a participant had decided that the purpose of the conversation they needed to have with a client was to discuss their strained relationship. But when he practised the conversation he realised that the relationship being strained was just his opinion; the content of the conversation he needed to have was about negotiating an effective price for the new year. These are very different purposes that would lead down very different paths. The 'strained relationship' was not a topic that the client had agreed to discuss. They thought that the issue was price as well. Phew!

4. Ask what is going on

This is a simple one but it's a goodie: it's effective when the person says one thing but you can see that there is something else going on. Their body language is the thing that normally gives them away. This is when we highlight what we see—not what we hear. For example:

- 'You say that you are okay but your body language tells me you are quite angry. Am I right?'

- 'From your lack of eye contact, you seem to be still unhappy. Is this the case?'

- 'You are saying you are fine but your eyes are welling up.' (I am pretty sure most of us will recognise the 'I'm fine' response if we have had any form of a relationship before.)

We state what we see (the power of facts) and then ask if there might be something more. We might acknowledge that we may not understand the full complexity of what is going on, but remain open to hearing more.

5. Get on the same page

Repeating what you are hearing or seeing, or summarising what the other person has said, is a very helpful way to help people feel heard and therefore safe. Whether you agree with what they are saying or not, it is about showing them that you are listening and interested. This could sound something like: 'Okay, so what I am hearing is that you are angry with Bill because he blamed you in front of a client. Is that a fair description of the situation?'

This technique can also be a good diffuser if what the other person is saying or doing appears to be unreasonable; for example, 'So what you have told me is that you did not meet the deadline because you saw that Sarah did not meet hers last week? Does that sound right?'

The only warning attached to this technique is that you need to be careful not to weave your opinions and feelings about what the other person is saying into the paraphrase. After all, they want to feel heard—not judged.

6. Make silence your friend

There is incredible power in shutting the hell up. This is very difficult for many people, but is incredibly powerful when someone is in fight mode, and especially powerful if they're in flight. Ask them a question and then wait for the answer. This is a very hard space for most people to be in; it's difficult for both the person being quiet and the person who's been asked the question — but it is an essential technique.

So many of us use silence as an excuse to keep pushing forward and talking through (or at) someone. Or we are so uncomfortable with the space that we fill in the gaps.

If someone is in flight mode, they don't want to contribute. They want to avoid, withdraw and retreat. If you fill the space then they will remain outside the safe zone and you will not be able to hear the real truth and reach a resolution.

If someone is in fight mode, it is the opposite. They are all about winning, so they will control and attack. The best thing you can do is let them run out of steam. They are more likely to be able to observe their own behaviours if you are being silent — there is no longer anyone to argue with.

When you become comfortable with silence, or even just practise it until you become friends, the benefits are tangible. You have the opportunity to see the other person's perspective, and let them feel heard and safe enough to return to a constructive conversation. When you are not talking it pushes others into having to share.

RESTORING SAFETY IS LIKE *pushing* THE BRAKES IN THE CAR. YOU ARE LESS LIKELY TO *crash*.

7. Validate their feelings

Let people know that it is okay to feel how they are feeling. The worst thing you can do is tell someone they should not feel the way they do. Has someone ever told you that you are being silly for feeling intimidated by them, or that you should not feel angry about a situation? How does it feel to be told that you should not feel a certain way? Frustrating, annoying, unheard—and yes, you can feel a little stupid or insecure as a result.

If people feel a certain way, let them. Don't tell others how they should feel. Allow them to feel, and they will feel safe enough to keep being honest with you.

If someone says they feel a certain way then repeating it back to them and validating their feelings creates a powerful connection. Phrases that are helpful include:

- 'I can see that this is a frustrating situation for you'
- 'I know you are annoyed'
- 'I understand how exhausting this must be'.

* * *

We now have these seven powerful techniques to restore safety in the conversation, so you can get back to having a constructive discussion.

Interestingly, restoring safety could actually take longer than discussing the actual content. So if you want the best outcome don't be in a rush to push through the content. Sometimes people need a while before they feel comfortable sharing with you and being honest with themselves. I have seen cases where people have not felt safe for up to 95 per cent of the conversation. But perseverance pays, and it becomes easier every time you need to give people feedback as trust and respect has been deepened.

When stalling is a good thing

We tend to associate stalling with delaying, avoiding, procrastinating or putting things off. How about we look at it in a different way? When can stalling be a good thing?

What about when you are stalling because it is preferable to making an error? You stall:

- the decision to pick up a cigarette until the urge passes
- the urge to call or text that person who is not good for you (we've all been there before)
- the urge to stop working on the proposal that is due in two hours
- your reaction to someone who has really set you off.

Stalling as a delaying tactic can be a good decision in some circumstances, especially when you are trying to break unhealthy or unhelpful habits, or when the reaction or action itself will be damaging and harmful to you and/or others.

In the context of managing yourself during stressful conversations or interactions, I propose that stalling can be good—if *really* necessary.

Thomas Paine, a writer said to have influenced the American Revolution, had it right when he said that 'the greatest remedy for anger is delay'. A moment of patience in a moment of anger saves you a hundred moments of regret.

Let's be clear here. Stalling a fight-or-flight reaction during a conversation is a good thing. The reaction doesn't lead to helpful behaviours, so put them off. This is quite different to putting off those things that are good for you. Things you want to *avoid* stalling include

- that workout you need to do
- telling someone you care about them
- seeing the specialist about a concern you have
- giving someone feedback they need to hear.

You just need to be honest enough with yourself to ask if stalling is your way of avoiding something that needs to happen.

Managing stress

When you are in a difficult conversation with someone (or with a group of people), you are the one in control of the moment (even though you may not feel like it). While you can't control others or the way they react, you can control your own thoughts and responses. Learning how to manage your own reactions can only have positive outcomes for everyone involved in the conversation.

In my workshops I've noticed that people seem to struggle to come up with a list of constructive ways to reduce their reactions in the moment. I have researched, and gathered through my own experience with people and cultures, a list of techniques that you can choose to own and practise.

- *Breathe*. Breathing slowly and consciously has a significant influence in calming the nervous system. The parasympathetic and sympathetic nervous systems work together to secrete hormones that reduce blood pressure and lower your heart rate. This calms the nervous system and therefore your reactions. Even the *way* you breathe is significant. When you breathe through your mouth it can trigger a fight-or-flight response. When you breathe with your mouth shut it promotes a sense of calm. This has a remarkable impact in the moment.

NEXT TIME YOU CAN *feel* YOURSELF GOING INTO *fight-or-flight*, JUST BREATHE.

- *Use positive self-talk*. The thoughts you feed yourself have a profound effect on your mental and physical wellbeing. If you feed yourself negative thoughts when you are stressed, what are you likely to hear? Yes, the negative thoughts; and that will send you on one quick downwards spiral and will not help the conversation. Whether the negative thoughts are focused on you or on others doesn't matter—they are not helpful at all.

Once you take a step back and look at your thoughts, you can then decide which ones are serving you and which ones are serving fear. Then you can decide which ones you will feed. No-one but you has control over your thoughts. So become a vigilant monitor when it comes to your thoughts, especially in those tough moments.

- *Be curious and ask open-ended questions.* Asking questions is good for a couple of reasons. It buys you time to help yourself calm down and stay in the conversation. It also shows you are interested in understanding, in hearing and seeing their perspective, and in developing an awareness of the 'real truth'.

  Questions that allow others to talk for a bit start with how, what and why, not 'do you', 'would you', 'can you'. These closed questions are likely to be met with a yes or no, rather than promoting further elaboration and conversation.

- *Ignore the story or speculation.* Chapter 4 looks at how damaging it is to lead with a story or speculate based on your own opinions and feelings. The key is to focus on the facts and tangible information, not on the stories in your head that, in fact, might not be true.

- *Listen deeply.* The greatest gift you can give someone is the gift of your attention. How does it feel when someone really listens to you? It makes a big difference. You need to become friends with silence for this to become easier. It does help to consider that if you speak you only enforce what you know; when you listen, you learn.

- *Go back to your notes.* There is nothing wrong with using notes for tough conversations. They ground you and allow you to stay on track. I still use notes for the tough ones, or when I find it hard to recall the exact facts. I say something like, 'Give me a sec to look back at my notes to make sure I am on track'. It's clear, explicit and true.

  So if you get lost, or find yourself in fight or flight, go back to the issue. What is it you were addressing? What are the facts? Stay on track this way.

* * *

If you want to get the best from a conversation you need to become ferocious at self-managing. After all, the only person you can really control is...yourself. So invest the time where it will have the greatest influence.

---

your CHeat sHeet

- Focusing on helping people feel safe in conversations is as important as the content itself.

- When people don't feel safe they have a natural fight-or-flight stress response that does not build relationships or encourage great decision-making.

- When you are in stress you are no longer at full capacity and can fail to hear the content or behave rationally.

- There are seven techniques that can move others to feeling safe:

  1 apologise, when appropriate

  2 make your comments about do and dont's

  3 gain agreement

  4 ask what is going on

  5 get on the same page

  6 make silence your friend

  7 validate their feelings

- The only time you should stall a conversation that needs to be had is when you might regret what you say or do.

- You need to become ferocious at managing your own fight-or-flight reactions to get the best out of the tough conversations.

Chapter 7
OWN YOUR STUFF

It's challenging for most of us to see who we really are and how we come across to others. Taking responsibility for the emotional wake that we leave behind when we treat people the way we do can be a daunting task.

I've heard people say, 'I don't care what people think of me'. That's rubbish. That's good old denial sitting in a protection mechanism. The thing is, they don't even know. It's not called denial for no reason.

The thing with self-awareness is that it is a very hard thing to define, and it is equally hard to achieve. Blind spots were appropriately named indeed.

We don't know what we can't see. When you choose to become more self-aware and to 'own your stuff', in and out of conversations, then you can watch your relationships grow, respect from others increase and productivity (yours and others') improve.

I have been told that I intimidate people. When I was first told this I was surprised. Were people intimidated because I appear confident and enjoy being in all types of situations? Was it because I give them feedback in the moment? Why should I be in the wrong for this? I was not up for hearing it at first, but when I thought about it I saw that it was a possibility. Even though I didn't want to admit it, it had become my blind spot. I had assumed that it was okay because my intent was usually good. But after some thoughtful reflection I chose to apologise to the two colleagues who felt I was intimidating. Then I refocused my style. I owned the fact that my intent wasn't always grounded in goodness. Sometimes I wanted to win and just get the bloody thing done.

I didn't stop having feedback conversations; I just had them with less gusto and more empathy. This small adjustment resulted in more enjoyable meetings and stronger relationships.

Being honest with yourself and owning your stuff really does make a difference, as confronting as it is.

The first challenge is to be courageous enough to own the wake we create and to understand the impact we have on others. The second is to do something about it. If we don't, we become our own roadblock.

Everyone has a story

It's all well and good to be self-aware, but it does not help us to understand *why* we might react the way we do, and think as we do. To understand this we can think of ourselves as an iceberg.

Generally we see only about 10 per cent of an iceberg when it is in the water. The rest is under the surface. The same can be said for the way others see us. There is so much more under our surface that has formed who we are. It's only our words, behaviours and physicality that people see and judge—and they do that pretty quickly. We need to be careful we don't fall into the trap of judging people as per the 'iceberg syndrome', as shown in figure 7.1.

Figure 7.1: the iceberg syndrome

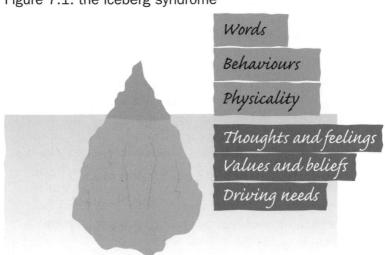

Words

Behaviours

Physicality

Thoughts and feelings

Values and beliefs

Driving needs

Let's uncover the elements of the iceberg syndrome.

Above the surface

- *People hear your words.* Whether they are harsh or soft, loud or quiet, abrasive or kind, conversations or 'yoursations', focused on gossip or maintaining integrity, or even whether they bring motivation to others or squash them, people hear your words.

- *People see your behaviours.* People notice if you are short-tempered, if you are a committed listener, if you are late to meetings, if you commit to deadlines, if you invest in those around you, if you are quick to judge or you seek the truth, if you do what you say or are all talk and little action.

- *People notice your physicality.* People notice your smile, or your frown, what you're wearing and your body shape. They even make assumptions about your race or religion. We are all born looking a particular way and belonging to a particular cultural group. This we can't change. Unfortunately we are often judged on it.

Under the surface

- *Our thoughts and feelings.* How we think and feel about things in our lives and the lives of others tends to dictate how we behave and react above the surface — that is, what people see and hear. If you think that you are ugly, it may be because kids at school said this to you, or it may be that the way you look was valued too much in your upbringing. Either way, you think your 'cover' will reflect this. You may not maintain eye contact with others, you may lack confidence and mumble your words, you may dress to disguise.

  If you feel frustrated and annoyed about your job, then you might be snappy and short-tempered in your interactions with your colleagues; you may have little tolerance for people going off track in meetings; you may drink too much at social occasions or blame people around you when things don't go right.

  How you think and feel dictates what you say and do. It's your thoughts and feelings that drive what people see. If you feel happy then you are often a pleasure to be around. If not, you need to be careful of your impact on those around you.

- *Our values and beliefs.* These are often formed very early on. They can be based on our cultural background or the people that we were around when we grew up. And there are so many variations within each of those alone. The values might vary from one culture being very direct to the other avoiding conflict.

  Another major influencer is people's spiritual beliefs and values. We know these are strong: many wars and atrocities occur in the name of religion. Or they can be formed simply from contact with the people we spend our time with. For example, one of my closest friends once invited a man named Jafar (who was a Hazari refugee from Afghanistan) to come and live with their family after reading about his story in the paper. As I got to know Jafar and his story it transformed what I believed and knew about Islamic culture; and hearing first-hand about his experiences living in a detention centre for more than two years changed my perspective on how we treat refugees. It's amazing how the stories that you choose to learn can influence your values and beliefs.

- *Our driving needs.* These may appear to be pretty simple. They are the *essentials* — the things that we need in order to survive, as proposed in 1943 by Abraham Maslow when he gave us Maslow's Hierarchy of Needs. He showed us that there are some priorities greater than others that shape our motivations. We need food and water; a roof over our heads; to be safe (both physically and psychologically); medicine to combat sickness; people to care for and care for us; and love.

  The driving needs of people in the Western world often look very different to those of people in developing nations. The things we think we need to survive can differ. The driving needs of someone in an 'unsafe' home will look very different to those of someone with a loving and stable home environment. Someone who has lived in a war-torn place or has survived a catastrophic event, such as a tsunami, will have a very different set of driving needs than an academic who grew up in an affluent suburb. If a war survivor is listening to an academic complain about the weather, or the poor coffee at the café, how do you think they will feel — or react?

When people with opposing feelings and thoughts, values and beliefs and driving needs operate in the workplace it is not easy. We all think we are right.

WHO TOLD YOU THAT YOUR *interpretation* OF LIFE IS THE RIGHT ONE?

Just like you, everyone has a story. We need to be very careful about judging others by what we see. It's like judging the book by the cover or the wine bottle by the label. We do it and we miss out as a result.

The colleague who spoke harshly to you this week may have something going on at home. The colleague who will not look you in the eye may come from a culture where direct eye contact is considered disrespectful; or maybe she lacks confidence because not enough people have invested in her. Or maybe she is intimidated by you.

The point is, you are only seeing 10 per cent of who people are. You don't know what's beneath the surface. People judge you in the same way. It's only when we are prepared to understand what is going on for each other under the surface that we have a good chance at collaborating well.

Beware of the Drama Triangle

When I attended Thought Leaders Business School one of the founders, Matt Church, presented a model called the Drama Triangle. It is a model of dysfunctional social interaction created by psychotherapist Stephen Karpman. Each point on the triangle, shown in figure 7.2, represents a common and ineffective response to conflict, one more likely to sustain dysfunction than to end it. The triangle can be used to help people understand the roles they play in situations that are not helpful, to themselves or others.

Figure 7.2: the Drama Triangle

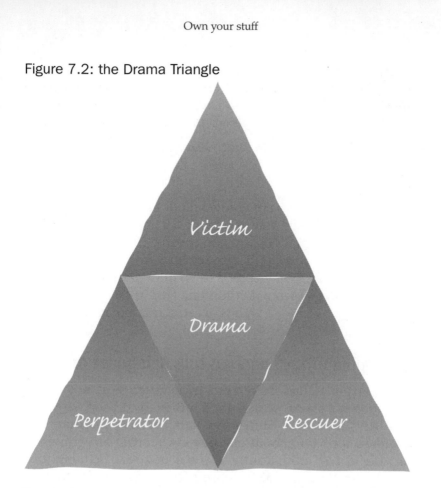

Participants in the Drama Triangle create dysfunction for themselves and those around them. Each person assumes a certain role.

The Victim

The Victim is helpless and hopeless. They deny responsibility for their negative circumstances, and are not open to the power to change them. They are hesitant or won't take a stand; they are very sensitive, think 'poor me', feel victimised and can assume impotence and incompetence. They will look for a rescuer that will support their negative feelings. If the Victim stays in this position they will block themselves from making productive decisions.

Examples of the Victim in the workplace might include the person who keeps saying yes to everything they are asked to do, which leads to an impossible volume of work to complete. Or the person who stays in a job they hate because there is no alternative—in their eyes.

The Rescuer

The Rescuer intervenes, seemingly out of a desire to help the situation or the Victim. They are constantly applying short-term repairs to a victim's problems, while neglecting their own needs. They are always working hard to 'help' other people. They are tired, and often have physical complaints. Rescuers may be angry underneath or be a loud or quiet martyr in style. They feel guilt if they don't rescue and can often keep the Victim dependent. They create unhealthy co-dependency roles.

The Rescuer is the least obvious role in the Drama Triangle. They are the person helping in the case of an emergency. They actually benefit from playing this role, as it plays to their ego or sense of self. They have a motive, seen or unseen, to feel better as a person. They play the role as a way of avoiding looking at their own anxiety and underlying feelings.

Examples of the Rescuer in the workplace include the person who jumps in and answers for others who have not delivered (and sometimes they even do their work). Or the person who keeps allowing the dysfunctional behaviours to occur because they are worried about the Victim. Or they are concerned about their wellbeing and worry that discussing the issue may challenge them too much. Rescuers find it very difficult to let others fail and learn from their mistakes.

The Perpetrator

The Perpetrator is the one who pressures, coerces or persecutes the Victim. They blame the Victim and criticise the enabling behaviour of the Rescuer, without providing guidance, assistance or a solution to the underlying problem. They are critical and unpleasant and good at finding fault. Perpetrators often feel inadequate underneath. They control with threats, order and rigidity. They can be loud or quiet in style, and can sometimes be a bully. They can be the 'critical' parent or boss.

The Perpetrator is easy to recognise in the workplace. They are the 'fighter'. They are the first to blame you for work not done well or to their standard, rather than offering solutions. This person might come up with phrases like, 'See what you made me do' and 'You got me into this mess'.

* * *

As transactional analyst Claude Steiner says, '... the Victim is not really as helpless as he feels, the Rescuer is not really helping, and the Persecutor does not really have a valid complaint'.

The Drama Triangle is sometimes referred to in the context of mind games: 'the unconscious games played by innocent people'. When you play any of these roles it takes you away from becoming more self-aware and does not allow you to own your stuff. Your interactions with others are tarred and finding ideal outcomes is near impossible. Aside from that, it's exhausting to play these roles for an extended period of time.

Think about some of the situations you find in your life that are not ideal, that play on your mind, or frustrate you. Are you playing any of these roles? What can you take ownership of?

Why we don't receive well

There's a reason we don't all run around asking for feedback. Most of us are committed to being a better version of ourselves, or at least a version that doesn't go around hurting others. But most of us are not that keen to know the truth about how others perceive us. We don't react well to feedback, so the best way to avoid the reaction is to not seek it out.

Getting feedback is tough for most of us. For high-performers, those truly committed to being the best, it's fuel. You wouldn't hear the fastest sprinter in the world, Usain Bolt, saying to his coach, 'Thanks Coach, but I've got it from here'. High achievers seek out feedback about their performance, and they do it often.

Thanks for the Feedback by Douglas Stone and Sheila Heen says there are typically three triggers that prevent people from receiving feedback well, or that cause them to block it. I think there are four.

1   *We have a 'truth' trigger.* This is when we are set off by the content itself. We don't like it, it might be false, we think it's untrue, unfair, unhelpful—and as a result we feel wronged, resentful and frustrated.

2   *We have a 'relationship' trigger.* This is when we have a reaction to the person giving the feedback. It might be they don't lead by example, they have no credibility, or that we simply don't like or respect them. We start to focus on the audacity of this person giving us the feedback.

3   *We have an 'identity' trigger.* This is when our reaction is not about the content or the person, but about how the feedback challenges our sense of self and who we are. It challenges our ego. We feel overwhelmed, threatened or ashamed. We get off-balance and question ourselves, and this is not a happy place.

4   *We have a 'delivery' trigger.* This is what I see a lot of, so I
    have added it. The giver might lead with their opinions and
    feelings without providing substantial examples; or it could
    be that what they say is correct but it is delivered in a harsh
    and disrespectful way.

The reason these triggers are challenging is not that they are
unreasonable or untruthful. They are not good because they
stop us from owning our stuff. We find an excuse not to accept
what is being shared with us. The challenge is to look to see if
our triggers are present and own the fact that we are choosing
not to receive the feedback well.

So how *can* we learn to receive the feedback well?

I wish it could be as simple as giving you this list of what you
need to do to receive feedback well, but we are complicated
beings. What I do know is that we can make choices all the time.

We can choose to stay in our trigger reaction (fight or flight)
and stay in the Drama Triangle and be the Victim and blame the
giver (the Perpetrator) — or we can recognise what is happening
and remind ourselves of these three things:

1   *Find the gold.* There is always something to learn from every
    conversation and interaction. We have to *choose* to find
    that piece of gold. It might be hidden deep, but it will be
    there. Learning to own our own stuff is key. After all, if a
    person has the courage to share (even if they do it poorly,
    or they are being a dick) then we should have the courage
    to question and try to understand the feedback — and
    ourselves in that process.

2   *Be the example.* Learn to manage your fight and flight
    reactions, in the moment. Lead by example by showing
    others how to react in difficult circumstances. You can't ask
    others to stay calm and reasonable and keep engaging if
    you can't do it yourself when challenged. 'Do as I say and
    not as I do' will not cut it if you want to become remarkable.

3   *Beware of the iceberg syndrome.* Remind yourself that others will only judge what you say and do — your 'above the surface' cover. So while your feelings, emotions, beliefs and values are bubbling under the surface, show them what you can be proud of — your words and behaviour.

We need to learn to finish conversations with 'Thanks for the feedback'. Not 'Thanks but ...'

Ego is a dirty word

Have you heard 'Ego is not a dirty word', a popular song by Skyhooks? If you are an Aussie over 40 years of age it's probably ingrained into your psyche. I propose the opposite of that song: ego *is* a dirty word. When our ego clouds our vision and our ability to see things clearly, it is no longer our friend. Ego holds us back from being a better version of ourselves, and stops us from building and maintaining respectful relationships.

Another word for ego is pride. For those of you thinking that some pride is good, you are right. There are actually two meanings of pride:

1   a sense of satisfaction in the achievements or actions of yourself or a group of people

2   an inflated sense of one's accomplishments or achievements.

We can see that the sort of pride described in the first definition is good. It is good to be satisfied with what we have done and achieved. There is no harm in a positive reflection on your efforts. You should be proud you received a good performance rating for the past six months when you worked hard; you should be proud your children are growing up to be thoughtful and considerate; you can be happy that the relationships around you are solid and can withstand the tough times.

The sort of pride described in the second definition is not good—it's too inflated and exaggerated.

I have had the pleasure of working with a funds management firm that teaches their clients how their thinking and beliefs influence poor decision-making. (Yes, you heard right. A funds management company that is genuinely interested in being transparent with its clients about investment decisions!) One of the messages the firm shares with its clients is that pride is not their friend. For example, sometimes people make some good or lucky decisions and think they have nailed the stock market. They can get a little cocky. They may become flippant with the next decision, or invest way too much in what looks like a sure thing, because they've 'got the touch'. News flash! If there was anyone who understood the complexities of the stock market inside-out they would be the richest person in history.

Pride and humility

It is the balance of pride and humility that makes for good relationships, opens the mind to new ways of thinking and helps us make better decisions as a result.

It is pride that has morphed into arrogance, without the relationship to humility, that causes problems. So ask yourself: where might you have an over-inflated view of yourself? Your capacity on the job, your role as a leader, your knowledge of a market or sector, your looks, what you own, how you make decisions...

Then ask yourself, how might your ego look to others? What might the impact be on other people, on your work, your decision-making, on your relationships?

The answers, while they might be hard to stomach, are great tools for personal change.

YOUR CHEAT SHEET

- When you become more self-aware and 'own your stuff', your relationships grow, respect from others increases and productivity improves.

- We're all a bit like icebergs: it is only our words, behaviours and physicality that others see and judge, but there is so much more under the surface that has formed who we are.

- It's only when we are prepared to understand what is going on for each other, under the surface, that we have a good chance at collaborating well.

- Participants in the Drama Triangle create dysfunction for themselves and those around them. Each person assumes a certain role. When you play any of these roles it takes you away from becoming more self-aware and does not allow you to own your stuff.

- There's a reason we don't all run around asking for feedback. We're not that keen to know the real truth about how others perceive us. We don't react well to feedback, so we do our best to avoid it.

- We all have triggers that prevent us from receiving feedback well. We need to recognise them and acknowledge that they're there if we are to move past them.

- We need to learn to finish conversations with 'Thanks for the feedback'. Not 'Thanks but …'

Chapter 8
THE Board OF Directors in your Head

Have you ever wondered why the same data can be presented to different people and result in many different perspectives and interpretations? This occurs because the way we interpret and receive information is unique to each of us.

When I was in my twenties I sat in one of my first leadership meetings where we were presented the strategy for the next financial year. We were shown a SWOT analysis (Strengths, Weaknesses, Opportunities, Threats), then a competitor analysis. After that we were shown the new products that were being launched and, to finish, we went through the budgets and forecasts. Everyone in the group was shown the same data. What happened next fascinated me. This was the first time in my career that I remember noticing that there were serious differences of opinion about the same information.

While there were definitely positive and supportive stances, what rang loudest for me were the more overtly expressed destructive perspectives. Some people found fault in every aspect they could find and saw mostly the negatives; some people focused on how risky the strategy was and the disasters that were likely to occur should they implement the strategy; and some people saw only good or bad and were not prepared to discuss the grey areas. There was also one person who, after the presentation, made their view very clear that the senior leadership team was to blame for not collaborating more effectively prior to the meeting and that if their leadership was better this would not have happened.

Yes, there might have been more consultation, or better presentation skills and even greater data analysis. But what surprised me the most was the plethora of dysfunctional reactions that made it difficult to discuss any feasible outcomes.

The way we perceive facts and react in situations is different for everyone. The mind is very powerful, and it can convince us of something that isn't necessarily true. But at the time we react, it is our truth, even if it is technically incorrect. For each of the people in the leadership meeting that day, their judgement of the strategy was the only true one. They could not see another perspective.

WE CAN BECOME OUR *own* COGNITIVE HAZARDS.

Even when we are all presented with the same information we see the truth very differently. These distorted perspectives can be like a 'mucus on our mind' that do not allow us to see a situation, person or perspective clearly. Or, like the crazy mirrors at the circus, they distort the way we see things.

The ten directors

When there is a distorted lens on the way we see things it causes what behavioural therapists call cognitive distortions (CDs). CDs are exaggerated or irrational thought patterns. They cause us to react to information, situations and people based on how *we* see them, and not in a good way.

Aaron Beck first proposed the theory behind CDs in 1972. Around 50 different kinds have been identified. There is a lot of detail to fathom and a lot of options for self-diagnosis.

Psychotherapist Matthew Cooksey and I have condensed them into ten groups:

1 Blamers

2 All About Me-ers

3 Black-and-White Thinkers

4 Negative Thinkers

5 Catastrophisers and Minimisers

6 Always Righties

7 The Powerless

8 Perfectionists

9 Labellers

10 The Entitled

These ten groups represent what we typically see in our own practices as distortions that prevent people from seeing the 'real truth'. Collectively, we call them the 'Board of Directors' that live in your head (or the BODs).

The Board of Directors becomes our blinkers. It's a set of blinkers on our mind that limits how much information or 'truth' we choose or are capable of seeing. I've got blinkers, you've got them, our colleagues have them and your partner is wearing them.

It's normal to have them. We all do. We just need to be aware of their impact and adjust our thinking and/or behaviour accordingly.

So how do we form these BODs? These things that rule how we perceive situations, information and relationships—and that then form our behaviours and actions? Let's have a look at members of the board first:

1. Blamers

A Blamer expects other people to change to suit them. They *need* others to change as their own happiness and satisfaction depends on it. Some Blamers think that if they cajole or pressure people enough they will change to suit their thinking. Some Blamers just blame in silence. Either way, whatever it is, it's not their fault.

Blamers hold others responsible for own their pain and/or frustrations. Statements such as 'It's not my fault I was late— my husband didn't set the alarm', and 'Stop making me feel like I'm doing a bad job' fall into this section.

Blamers tend to be relaxed when people around them are doing what they want them to do, in the way they want them to do it. But they get stuck in the 'blame trap' when things don't go their way. This trap does not allow them to see their contribution to the situation. Blamers often feel that someone has made them behave in a particular way, rather than admitting or indeed realising that they chose that reaction themselves. For example, a Blamer may say that a person 'made me frustrated because of how annoying they were'. But no-one *makes* you experience an emotion, such as frustration. You *choose* to be led by it.

GETTING STUCK IN BLAME IS LIKE DRINKING A BOTTLE OF *poison* IN THE HOPE THAT IT WILL KILL YOUR ENEMIES. IT'S A TOXIC BEHAVIOUR THAT *damages* RELATIONSHIPS AND PRODUCTIVITY IN THE WORKPLACE.

Let's look at a day in the life of a Blamer. We will call him Barry.

Barry has just missed the tram. It pulled off 20 seconds before he reached the door. If the tram driver hadn't been in such a rush then he wouldn't be late. He gets into work and goes to make a cup of coffee, but the milk is empty. Even though it is his week to stock the fridge, someone should have reminded him. How is he supposed to remember otherwise?

Barry has been working on a new product for over six months now and it hasn't been easy. The problem is that people don't read the instructions properly. After all, he wrote a 25-page document to explain what he needed ... he says it's very clear. It's been really hard to get everyone together, as well. Why does Sharon have to take Fridays off? It's his best thinking and strategising day, and if the team wants the best from their project manager they should work around him, after all.

After a long day with many frustrations (normal) he arrives home to no heating. What the? If his wife had considered the possibility that it could fail during this cold, cold winter then she could have organised for it to be serviced. He's going to bed early tonight anyway, because his ankle is sore from spraining it while running for the tram. Bleeping tram driver!

The sad truth for Barry and other Blamers-by-nature is that while it's the fault of their mother, their father, their boss and the government that they are unhappy, frustrated, annoyed or upset, Blamers will remain trapped in their own thinking. They find it very difficult to find happiness and learn from experience. More importantly, it makes it harder to find the lesson about themselves that will help them move forward and become a better version of themselves.

Perhaps Barry could consider the sage advice from the Dalai Lama: 'It is far more useful to be aware of a single shortcoming in ourselves that it is to be aware of a thousand in somebody else'.

2. All About Me-ers

For All About Me-ers everything others do or say is a direct reaction to something they have said or done or omitted to say or do. The outcomes can be positive or negative.

At the core of All About Me-ers there is an excessive concern for self (and about how others perceive that self) and for their own reputation. Everything that happens around them, and to them, can be directly attributed back to them. All About Me-ers tend to magnify their part in other people's lives and circumstances; therefore the focus is more on them than on those around them.

Their emotional climate is often rooted in a level of pride and arrogance or in shame and insecurity. It's all about what they did or did not do. For example, an All About Me-er would have no doubt that their colleague got that recent promotion because of the time and attention they'd invested in that colleague (pride and arrogance). An All About Me-er would be sure that their sister lost her job because they didn't have the conversation with her about how late she is all the time. If only they had told her sooner it would not have happened (shame and insecurity).

It's all about them ... and they just can't see that. It's like playing in a doubles tennis match and considering that any win or loss comes as a direct result of your performance (not your partner's).

Let's take a look at Mary, who sees the 'Me' in most things.

Mary struggles to have conversations without assuming they are all about her. Just the other day one of Mary's good friends mentioned how lucky she was to have such a committed, compassionate partner who is always looking for ways to make her happy. Mary's immediate response was, 'I do things to please him too, you know'. Mary assumed her friend was saying that she is not an equal in the relationship. No, Mary. She was just saying your partner is a great person. Full stop.

Mary tends to make most things about her, and from her perspective it's the only way she has of measuring things. The problem is exacerbated by the fact that she has a job where comparison is the norm. She's in a state-based sales role, and every day the sales figures come in and get reported back to the team nationally. While she tends to fall into the top 20 per cent of salespeople, she knows she could be better but just doesn't have people skills that some of her colleagues do. If only she had the gift of the gab, she could be better. She just knows that every time the sales figures come out she will need to do more to become a great performer. It's hard for her to just celebrate where she is at. There's a reason they say that comparison is the killer of joy.

It's hard for Mary, though. She knows that what she does, or doesn't do, affects others all the time. For example, at work today the accounts guy was clearly struggling with the volume of orders he had to process. Mary knew that if she had held back and given him her orders over a few days that he would be coping better. Why didn't she think?! (Little did she know that he was just struggling with a new software program and his computer had been freezing all day. Nothing to do with Mary's orders.)

Oh, Mary. She's always trapped in her own thinking that most things are about what she has or hasn't done.

3. Black-and-White Thinkers

Black-and-White (B&W) Thinkers polarise their own thinking. They think in absolutes and extremes. It's perfect or terrible. It's ideal or it's horrendous. There is very little middle ground. If they don't do something really well then they consider it to be a total failure. It's the failure to bring both negative and positive qualities of themselves and others into a realistic whole. They are not comfortable with the grey areas. Grey areas are not okay and not an option they entertain.

B&W Thinkers operate like a swinging pendulum. They swing from one opinion to another without allowing themselves to sit comfortably in the middle. The following words are warning signs that this sort of thinking might be happening:

always	never	perfect
impossible	awful	terrible
ruined	disastrous	furious

Bobby considers himself pretty self-aware and is passionate about the people he has in his life and the impact he has on them. He woke on this one morning and it was grey outside, and he decided that it was going to be a tough day.

The first email of the day was the report back from Risk about the issues associated with implementing Project Accelerate. There were more than five stated risks out of 25 potentials. His first thought was, 'We need to drop the project. It just won't work'. He took this thinking to the team meeting that morning.

The team had other ideas. They discussed using these highlighted risks to re-do the implementation strategy for an even better version of the project. Bobby couldn't see how it would work, because there was no guarantee it would eliminate the potential risks. They were at a stalemate.

His wife called him that day. She had to get back to her cousin about whether they would meet them for the weekend. His wife said she felt unsure. Bobby said that meant they should not go. No need to discuss it further. You either want to go or you don't. If you can't decide, it's a no. (Well, in his mind anyway.)

One of Bobby's team members came to him that afternoon with an idea. Bobby could not see how it would work. He did not give approval as it was clear it was going to fail. 'Where's the middle ground to discuss it?', his team member wondered.

Imagine having a discussion with Bobby about politics or religion? No thanks.

4. Negative Thinkers

These thinkers take negative information, magnify it and filter out all the positives. They pick pieces of information and dwell on them so their perspective becomes darkened or distorted. They are generally glass-half-empty people.

Negative Thinkers tend to say no to things before they have even properly considered them. They think it won't work, there's no point, or it's too hard. These people can be particularly challenging in a work or team environment.

When there are two perspectives to take, Negative Thinkers will always side with the negative; they often call themselves 'realists', but really they are pessimists. People tend to stay away from Negative Thinkers, as they have a problem for every solution.

Negative thinking is cognitive suicide. Did you know that for the average person 80 per cent of habitual thoughts, the ones we ruminate on, are negative? Dr Daniel Amen, a world-renowned psychiatrist and brain-imaging specialist, tells us that most people have more than 45 000 negative thoughts each day. These thoughts don't always present as doomsayer thinking. They can just be doubt, disappointment, blame, frustration, stress, dislike or just plain apathy.

So if you are thinking this type of thinking does not apply to you, think again. There is statistical certainty that you are highly influenced by those negative thoughts.

Let's look at Negative Thinker Neil's story to get a clearer understanding.

Neil has just finished reading the last month's company report. The company may as well shut up shop now. As the company's accountant, it is his role to be the realist when looking at the numbers and the future of the business. Neil can't believe that the company has lost one of their biggest accounts. They have been supplying to ABC Ventures since the day they set up eight years ago. ABC Ventures has been hard work when it comes to chasing payment; in fact, Neil had to hire another Accounts person to chase the debt. But ABC does account for 15 per cent of the income.

Never mind that the profit increase for the month was 4 per cent. That will be eaten away in the next few months with all the money that needs to be spent on upgrading the IT systems. There is no way they will be able to recover from this.

Neil picks up the phone to the operations manager to discuss. 'I think this is one of the worst months we've ever had. I think we need to reconsider our future.' The ops manager is confused: 'Neil, we're at final stages and highly likely to take over the biggest account in the region; we've just heard we have renewed three contracts; and in two weeks we have our new CEO from our biggest competitor starting. The news is good. What's the problem?'

'Have you got your head in the sand?', Neil retorts. 'You are being totally unrealistic about what's ahead of us and it's getting tiring being the doomsayer around here.'

You're telling me, Neil.

5. Catastrophisers and Minimisers (C&Ms)

Catastrophisers and Minimisers (C&Ms) maximise or minimise issues. They see information and situations as much larger or less significant than they actually are. Similar to B&W Thinkers, there is no middle ground on issues that need addressing. C&Ms either make things into a big drama or they downplay the severity of a situation.

C&Ms expect disaster to strike anytime or they inappropriately shrink the magnitude of the impending event. They hear about a problem and tend to go through a lot of what-ifs ('What if it happens to me?', 'What if it gets worse?') or, on the other side of the spectrum, they brush it off ('It's not a biggie', 'No need to even discuss it really').

As a Catastrophiser, Caren loves a bit of drama and she's mates with Marie, a Minimiser who likes to underplay situations.

Caren has heard that her daughter has been poorly for a few days and is really annoyed she did not let her know. Caren calls her daughter: 'OMG, OMG ... I'm coming over immediately. I will drop over meals for a week. I have called the doctor and he is on standby in case things get worse. I'm not discussing this ... you should have told me. What if you get pneumonia?'

Caren can't believe her daughter did not let her know earlier. These illnesses can turn in minutes, so she really needs to be on top of it.

Just yesterday she was having to restore a situation for her friend Marie. Marie had an informal conversation with her manager about how her performance needs to improve. Marie said things will be fine, because other people in the office have had similar conversations. Marie's decided to put it to the side, as others have it worse. Caren can't believe it. She thinks Marie needs to start looking for another job, call the bank and ask them for an extension on her loan, start selling some items on eBay to store up some cash and get some counselling to be able to deal with the future rejection.

Some people just don't think about the real risks, Caren says to herself. Marie can't believe this warrants any attention. It'll be fine.

6. Always Righties

Always Righties (aka Righties) are continually on a mission to prove that what they say and what they do is correct. I'm right, you're wrong, the end. There are no other potential conclusions.

Righties need to win, regardless of the cost. They will often go to great lengths to demonstrate their 'rightness', including hurting people they love. These people are not big on apologies, as they don't feel they are necessary or warranted. Being wrong is unlikely and unpalatable to a Rightie, and not something they like to contemplate. They can be difficult to be around. In extreme cases they are stubborn, combative, disruptive, arrogant, self-centred and rude.

When having a conversation, Righties struggle to listen effectively to all the content because they are busy selecting evidence to build their case. They are many steps away from the 'real truth' in discussions, because their opinion is the only one that counts.

Over many years of being a practising Rightie they can start displaying an oppositional reflex. This is observed as the automatic impulse to do or think the exact opposite of what is being suggested or discussed. That means that no matter what the issue is, their instinctive response is oppositional.

'I'm not arguing. I'm explaining why I'm correct.' If you resonate with this statement then chances are you may have a need to be right. One of the best relationships Righties can have is with themselves. Unfortunately, being a Rightie is a fast track to a life of professional and personal isolation. It also stifles creativity and innovation, as it does not allow for others' opinions and ideas.

Let's have a look at Ron, who has been a senior executive for many years now. Ron knows his stuff in the engineering space. Ron is one of the experts. Or so Ron tells us. In fact, Ron's knowledge is astounding. He knows the best party to vote for, that Paris is better to travel in than Spain (even though he hasn't been to Spain), and how to bring up children (especially other people's). He can back it all up with facts and opinion. You don't even have to ask him.

Working on strategy with Ron should be easy, he thinks. He asks for a couple of ideas and then he just knows the best direction. It would be much faster if people just agreed and got on with it. The discussions frustrate him. The same happens at home with his wife. Just last week he researched and found the best place to eat in their area. He knows where they should go. His wife has been there and didn't find it that impressive. Well, Ron knows because he found it on Google. He told his wife she just didn't order the right dish.

The last dinner party they had Ron ended up in a heated discussion with his guests about the cause of the GFC. He had to let them know they were 'ignorants, with a limited education and unlikely to see a sabre-toothed tiger if it was sitting at the table with them'. He doesn't know why they got so sensitive and left early.

The trouble with Ron is that he thinks everyone else has no idea. But who's the common denominator here?

7. The Powerless

Powerless people can also be known as victims. They can have a 'poor me' mentality. They have endless tales of woe and tragic stories about things that have happened to them through no fault of their own. Powerless mentality is like standing in the rain, getting wet and wondering why the weather is against you.

The Powerless feel situations and circumstances are out of their control and unwittingly give up their capacity to get a better outcome, or to own their part. They have elected to give up ownership of their circumstances but can fail to see how they do this.

Powerless people can feel responsible for the pain and happiness of others ('Why aren't you happy? Is it something

I said or did?', or 'I shouldn't have bought that dinner for you. You wouldn't have food poisoning otherwise.'). In this place people often *should* all over themselves, because they have a list of what they should and should not do ('I must' or 'I ought to'. 'I should do this. I should not do that.'). Their emotional conscience is guilt.

Penny is exhausted. She's been working 16-hour days for more than four months now and it's getting harder and harder to get up in the mornings, let alone do the power thinking she needs to. The problem is that she is the only one that knows what needs to be delivered and it's just faster if she gets on with it.

Penny delivered an incredible report to the client last week and thinks that this will get the business over the line with the next piece of work. In the meantime, she is working with three other clients and training two new staff members. Her boss told her she should be the one to work on the next 'client pitch' so she better get on to that soon too. She feels bad she has not been able to devote as much time to the new people as she should.

To make things worse, Penny gets home to a mess ... she should have cleaned up last night but the kids were doing her head in. If she spent more time with them they would be easier to manage. She feels terrible that her daughter had to put her project in late and will have a mark deducted. If she were home more often that would not have happened. She really should devote more time to the family. It's just that she has to work, as no-one else will do it. If only she could clone herself. Penny wishes things were different.

I think Penny would benefit from the advice of Eckhart Tolle, a popular spiritual author from the USA: 'When you complain, you make yourself a victim. Leave the situation, change the situation or accept it. All else is madness'.

8. Perfectionists

Perfectionism is not about being perfect, but striving for it. It may not involve all elements of life but it will influence several aspects, be it work, sport, relationships or study. Perfectionism has a few dimensions, including:

- the relentless pursuit of extremely high standards, for yourself and others

- judging your self-worth based largely on your ability to achieve the high standards you have set

- experiencing the negative consequences of setting such demanding standards, yet continuing to go for it despite the personal costs.

Comparing themselves, or those around them, to others can become the norm for perfectionists. There may be an element of ranking, which is when a person draws unnecessary comparisons between individuals or groups for the purpose of raising their own self-esteem or lowering someone else's.

Ultimately, perfectionism is an unattainable goal that can end up being a noose around a person's sense of self, their happiness and their satisfaction in relationships. The phrase 'comparison is the thief of joy' is well known for a reason. It's true!

Peter is committed to being the best he can be. He wants to make sure that every presentation he does is flawless, with brilliant layout and no idea left unconsidered. He keeps working on them up until ten minutes before he is due to present; he usually discovers a mistake and is not able to relax, nor be satisfied with what he has done well.

Peter's team knows that they need to be careful when they come to Peter with an idea or concept. There is no point discussing it unless they have considered all potential variables. So they slowly stop coming with new things, yet he doesn't realise it.

Peter has his performance review to prepare for next week. He's not feeling confident in his work so he just rates himself below average for all areas. The discussion is clearer that way, as he knows he has work to do. Peter's wife reminds him that in the whole time she has known him his leaders have always acknowledged him as a high achiever. She suggests maybe it's time for him to accept that he will never get things 100 per cent correct, and just enjoy the journey.'As if', he thinks.

9. Labellers

Labellers have an unhelpful thinking style that makes generalisations or judgements about themselves or others, based on just one or two behaviours.

A typical Labeller will drop something on the floor and label themselves as clumsy. Or they miss a deadline and tell themselves they are hopeless. When focused on others, a Labeller will see a colleague speaking poorly to one of their team members and then decide that she is a bully. Or a customer does not call them back and they label them disrespectful.

Labelling is not an uncommon way of thinking, and it can be easy to fall into. The real damage occurs when a Labeller decides that someone (or themselves) *is* that type of person. They label themselves as clumsy or hopeless. Or they label the other person as a bully or disrespectful. They then treat themselves or the other person accordingly.

Instead of the error or behaviour being treated in isolation, in the context of a particular situation, Labellers affix a very sticky label onto themselves or the other person. Those labels can be difficult to remove.

Lesley has just finished meeting with her new client. She knew he was going to be a control freak from the first interaction, when he dismissed her suggestion to do the update reports weekly. In the meeting today he tried to steer the agenda and get everything his way again. Lucky she is on to his type.

At least Lesley has her new boyfriend she can vent to. From the day she met him she knew he would be trustworthy. It's really surprising that he has let her down on a couple of issues where his version of the truth was different to hers, but since he is trustworthy she's decided she won't worry about this.

Lesley's quick assumptions and labelling of the people in her life, whether right or wrong, may get her into trouble. She decides a person is a certain type of person, and she will look for information to support that claim in all interactions. (I would suggest it is healthier to consider each situation in isolation for the moment.)

10. The Entitled

Entitlement mentality is an unrealistic, unmerited or inappropriate expectation of favourable treatment from others, or of favourable living conditions. It is a way of looking at life where people believe they are *owed* things, irrespective of whether they work for them.

The Entitled may believe they are deserving because of who they are, or where they live, or the job they have. They can be associated with statements such as:

* 'I shouldn't have to do this'
* 'I shouldn't have to pay for this'
* 'The company owes me'.

The Entitled can make a workplace, relationship or home very difficult to be in, as they are not geared to working towards gaining anything—whether it be a promotion, money or even relationships with people. It is like creating a dream or vision of your future and believing it should be come easily to you.

Eddie has been in this job for over eight years now, longer than most of the employees. According to him, he has also negotiated some of the best deals the business has ever had. He is struggling to come to terms with the fact he has not been offered better options for when the company publicly lists. On top of that he had to wait three months to receive access to the company car park when he bought a car this year. At least the car dealership treated him with respect and turned on the attention when he was there.

It's not just work that is unfair. Even his favourite restaurant, which he has introduced many people to, is not able to open one hour early for drinks for his birthday. Seriously? He has invested a lot of time and money in that place.

He can look on the bright side. When the national sales manager leaves next month he is clearly going to be offered that role, and he'll get that pay rise he deserves.

People are not aware of their BOD thinking habits

We have been programmed to a way of thinking based on our education, upbringing, beliefs, religion and experiences. This distorts how we view the world, including the people around us and the situations we find ourselves in. (If you think you are blinker-free and immune to your own 'dysfunctional' thinking because you know best, then you may fall into the 'Always Right' category of thinking.)

CHANGING HOW WE THINK IS NOT AS SIMPLE AS *deciding* TO DO SO. WE NEED TO *understand* WHERE OUR THINKING AND JUDGEMENTS WERE SEEDED SO WE CAN *reframe* OUR THINKING FOR THE BETTER.

We need to change our thinking and our BODs to change our behaviours. As a child I was told that voting for a particular party was the only way. When I became an adult my first vote was for the party that was ingrained in my belief system. No-one could convince me of a different way. It was only when I did my own research, and had my own experiences, that I felt comfortable enough to make a decision that differed from my parents'.

We tend to think that the way we think is the right way. It might be the case, but more often than not it is based on our perceptions and those experiences and lessons we have had.

BOD thinking leads to poor decisions

If we only ever see our own perspective, without removing the BODs, we are at serious risk of making poor decisions that could pose a high risk and lead to serious consequences.

In my days as an HR manager I used to coordinate and attend biannual human capital meetings. This forum provided a structure for assessing people's performance in a matrix-based organisation. When people have multiple reporting lines the performance management process becomes more complicated. By gathering all the relevant people in the room to discuss an individual, we were able to collate the feedback about the employee for their manager to give them directly.

This structure proved the most efficient way to collate feedback and then make a group assessment on the individual's performance. The process had many benefits, but at the same time it had its flaws. One project director might think the individual's ability to produce reports was outstanding, 'just amazing'; and another might think they were well below average, as they missed a piece of data and had the wrong client heading on a page. At a glance, this could be a Maximiser and a Negative Thinker at play. Two people see the same situation yet have very different perspectives.

The consequences for the employee in question could be wide-ranging in terms of performance rating, bonus, promotion, respect from their colleagues or at worst a job loss. The outcome could easily be based on poor decisions based on how *we think*, not on how *they perform*.

The good news is evidenced when I worked with an impressive financial services organisation where we ran a whole-of-company 'remarkable communication' program. All employees learned about their BODs and the power of separating facts from opinions and stories. One of the outcomes from the program was that their human capital day was the shortest they'd ever had and there was more agreement than ever before. The leaders learned that their flawed thinking patterns got in the way of assessing people's real performance. People received bonuses and promotions based on shared thinking and examples, not on the leaders' perspectives of their teams' performance. Powerful stuff.

Removing the BODs is not about getting everyone on the same page. As we know, that is one of the biggest killers of innovation and creativity. Often, disagreement and healthy conflict are the birthplace of creativity. This is about removing the unhealthy filters that cause us to see things through a blurred lens.

BOD thinking leads to poor relationships

Our dysfunctional thinking can draw us away from collaborative work and great relationships with others.

There was a client I coached a few years ago, who was the national sales manager of a consulting business. One of the issues he wanted to work through was how to renegotiate a new contract with a longstanding customer. In his eyes, the customer was 'being far too unreasonable and practically asking for a free ride'.

Without going into detail, my client provided a new contract and terms. He had spent considerable time thinking about the best possible solution and how to make it price-competitive. His customer came back with a counteroffer. The manager was insulted and decided that he was offering the initial contract, or nothing. As far as he was concerned he had offered a very good deal based on the customer's loyalty and outstanding credit record.

Now I can already hear those of you with sales and customer relations experience cringing. Yes, we all know that relationships are two-way and should be built on respect. But if we are honest with ourselves we don't always walk in the other person's shoes. My client had done the thinking and offered the best possible solution. There was nothing better (B&W thinking). He was right (Always Right thinking). His customer was the problem (Blamer thinking). And then he led with that when he spoke to his customer.

How do you think that conversation went? How do think the relationship was after? Correct. Not exceptionally good.

My client bravely accepted that his judgements were not helping the situation and that they had led to a damaged relationship. The good news is that he went back to his customer with an apology and they got started on the renegotiation. Thankfully, the customer was open to forgiveness.

∗ ∗ ∗

Go back to the ten BODs and select three that you can relate to. Consider when they might create flawed thinking. Then, think about the impact that has on your relationships and how you work.

The BODs are very loud and very persuasive lifelines to happiness or depression. After all, as Anaïs Nin said,'We do not see things as they are. We see them as we are'.

Being aware of the BODs that hinder our ability to see things clearly is one thing. Leading yourself out of the BOD thinking trap is the next challenge, and I suggest some tools for this in chapter 9.

YOUR CHEAT SHEET

- We all develop unhealthy and unhelpful thinking patterns that affect how we view people, situations and data. We form this thinking based on our experiences and understandings. They are distortions that hold us back from seeing the 'real truth'. We are often not even aware of them.

- These thinking patterns explain why one person sees a glass half-full and other sees it as half-empty. Or you see clear water and the other sees dirty. It's the same glass of water; we just have very different perspectives.

- There are up to 50 cognitive distortions identified. We call them the Board of Directors (BODs) that live in your head. They are:

  1 Blamers

  2 All About Me-ers

  3 Black-and-White Thinkers

  4 Negative Thinkers

  5 Catastrophisers and Minimisers

  6 Always Righties

  7 The Powerless

  8 Perfectionists

  9 Labellers

  10 The Entitled

- BODs can often lead to poor decision-making, as they influence the way we see situations and the people around us.

- BODs can lead to poor relationship-building, as they can pull us away from collaborating and learning to appreciate difference.

Chapter 9

CLIMB OUT OF THE THINKING TRAP

As explained in chapter 8, we all have unhealthy thinking patterns that affect how we make decisions and build relationships. Accepting and acknowledging them is the first step. The next is choosing to take some action and climb out of the thinking traps we can so easily fall into.

There are some tools that are well-suited to managing individual BODs; in this chapter, without being too specific I highlight the main ones that typically result in significant shifts in thinking and behaviours.

Stay in your lane

Imagine if we chose to own our part of every interaction we had? While the term 'stay in your lane' is not new, it first became known and real to me when I was a participant in a program called Insight run by Bev McInnes. Insight was a program aimed at understanding how our behaviours and mindsets are affected by what has happened to us during our life.

Insight was specifically focused on painful circumstances or experiences that we have gone through—whether we were conscious of this pain or not, it needed more digging. It was a full-on program in terms of the vulnerability it required, but it was life-changing at the same time.

One of the premises of the program was the need for us to focus on how our experiences affected *us* personally. Not how they changed our brothers, or sisters, or parents or carers, or those around us.

It wasn't about trying to analyse why the person who affected us did what they did. It wasn't about having 'aha' moments about the experiences that led to our partner or children seeing things the way they see them. We needed to stay in *our own* lane: to mind our own business and stay in our own traffic, not veer into other people's lanes and steer their traffic. (Although, I must say it did help me see why people are the way they are.)

People often veer out of their lanes. You might be reading an article, for example, and come across a section about the need to listen to other people if they are to feel valued. As far as you're concerned, that section practically highlighted itself red and applies directly to your manager. You can't wait to give her the book so she can own it.

This is not minding your own business. This is not staying in your own lane.

Good friends of mine, Chris and Lynne Burgess, have five adult children and have been married for over 35 years. According to Lynne, who is the author of *All in Night* and has given workshops on parenting and marriage, those years of marriage have not been easy. Lynne talks about one of the turning points in the marriage, when they moved from 'blame', and the 'it's *you* that needs to change' mentality, to working on themselves. She and Chris focused on owning their reactions to each other, and focused on staying in their own lanes. Yes, marriage is still a challenge for everyone, but their secret has been inspiring to me and to many others. 'A healthy, lasting relationship can only be built between two people who daily choose one another and take full responsibility for that.'

When in a conversation with another person and you feel your fight-or-flight stress reactions rising, maturity says 'Okay. I am reacting here. What can I own?' *Then* focus on the other person and their impact. I'm not saying people don't have their stuff and that it's not relevant. What I'm saying is, if you wish to maintain connection with others then look at managing yourself first, and *only then* at the other person.

Offence, disappointment, resentment and blame are emotions that all leaders (of people, ideas and concepts) need to deal with to become remarkable.

Staying in your lane is about owning the learning or the change that *you* need to own. It's about climbing out of the blame trap, where everybody else needs to work on their stuff. If you want to be the change you want to see ... then be it. Own it. Shift the burden to yourself. Otherwise you stay in the Drama Triangle (see figure 7.2 on p. 105) and nothing moves forward. And the Board of Directors continues to thrive.

Learn to recognise and replace your thinking

Before you drive any change and replace bad habits for better ones you need to have the intention to notice the thoughts and thinking patterns that come into your head. Are you observing the facts or are you ruminating on your opinions and feelings? Are you feeding information that might not be correct? Are you blowing things out of proportion? Are you still in fight-or-flight mode? Are you busy being right or downplaying the situation?

The reticular activating system (RAS) is a tiny but extremely hardworking part of your brain that filters enormous amounts of incoming information and draws your attention to anything important. When you decide to notice something you're telling the RAS that it's important. Have you ever booked a trip and then suddenly noticed your holiday destination popping up in overheard conversations, in the media—in the novel you're reading?! That's the RAS working its magic.

Be intentional about noticing your thoughts and the RAS will bring unhealthy thinking to your attention. Use it as a trigger for re-programming more useful thinking.

Smile

Do you have someone in your world that seems to be always smiling? I do. In fact, I'm blessed with a few of them. Even when things aren't going their way they still smile through it. Both of my children's grandmothers are serial smilers. It's no surprise that my kids love being around them, and that their lives are full of people who are drawn to them.

Smiling has a proven effect on the health and wellbeing of ourselves and others. In 1974 psychologist James Laird discovered that there is a difference between fake and real smiles. He showed that the real smiles (the ones with our eyes, not just the ones where we move our mouth in an upward fashion to impersonate a smile) do make a difference. In saying that, there is even some research to suggest that fake smiles can turn into real ones, just by the very nature of giving them a go.

There are numerous proven benefits to smiling. Genuine smiling can:

- boost your immune system through the release of serotonin
- lower your blood pressure
- change your interactions with others for the better
- build better relationships with your colleagues, customers and those around you as people are drawn to you
- make you more attractive. (It's true! Compare yourself when expressionless to a smiley face. It's just so much better.)

How good is it that smiling can be an antidote for unhappiness, stress and anxiety? It's simple and it costs us nothing. I am a serial smiler and I say it is a no-brainer.

Build a community of positive people

The people we hang out with influence how we think and feel.

We spend a lot of time trying to find our tribe, a group of people where we feel we fit and are valued. I can still remember the angst and stress of making friends at school and then the relief of finally finding a place where I was accepted. The people you spend your time with either build your sense of self or deplete it. I recall a past relationship that was so soul-destroying that it took me considerable time to rebuild the way I thought about myself and what I deserved in life. However, I chose to allow that person in, and I certainly chose to stay in that relationship, so I am not blaming—just observing the impact the wrong people in your life can have.

In some circumstances you may not have the luxury of choosing your tribe. The workplace is a great example of this. Poor cultures can be as toxic as poor friendships. If the majority of the people (after all, it is a group of people that contribute to a culture) bring you down with negativity or lack of support then this will of course affect your happiness.

The same goes for those you choose to have in your life—those people you invest your time in outside of work. Surround yourself with good people who are going to be honest with you and look out for your best interests, and not just people who tell you what you want to hear. The honest ones are the gems.

It is helpful to ask yourself these questions regularly:

- Who am I around?
- What are they doing for me?
- What have they got me reading?
- What have they got me saying?
- Where do they have me going?
- How do they have me thinking?
- What do they help me become?

By the same token, ask yourself about your own contribution to the lives of the people around you: it's only fair and fruitful when you are able to reciprocate and fill their joy tanks as much as they yours.

Feed the good wolf

This is a simple one but it is my absolute favourite. It doesn't need any explaining. Here's how Marci Shimoff tells it in her book *Happy for No Reason*:

> One evening a Cherokee elder told his grandson about the battle that goes on inside people. He said, 'My son, the battle is between the two "wolves" that live inside us all. One is Unhappiness. It is fear, worry, anger, jealousy, sorrow, self-pity, resentment and inferiority. The other is Happiness. It is joy, love, hope, serenity, kindness, generosity, truth and compassion'.

> The grandson thought about it for a minute and then asked his grandfather, 'Which wolf wins?'

> The old Cherokee simply replied, 'The one you feed.'

Feed the good wolf.

Look for the gift

Many years ago I was told by someone I did not respect that I was too picky when I passed judgements and that I did not give people enough time to process problems or situations. Of course there were no examples provided, and the delivery was like being hit by a freight train. It was something along the lines of, 'Georgia, you don't respect others' ideas enough when working through issues and you need to learn how to collaborate'.

Okay, so many issues here. As explained in chapter 7, we can have reactions to feedback on many levels. Here were mine.

1 *Content trigger.* Initially I did not believe the information I was given. Without any examples it certainly made it hard to understand the context.

2 *Relationship trigger.* I did not respect or trust the person who was giving me the feedback. I was aware that some of my colleagues felt the same, so I felt justified in refuting his feedback.

3   *Identity trigger.* This feedback challenged the way I saw myself as a leader in the business. I felt I had a good grasp on working in teams. I certainly made mistakes, but I valued my colleagues' ideas.

4   *Delivery trigger.* The way he said it was not cool. It was all opinion, and the tone was quite accusatory.

I would have been quite justified in discounting that feedback completely. But when you stay in the blame trap or the Drama Triangle you can't learn from a situation or see the facts clearly. If you are blaming the person, the content, the way the person made you feel, their perspective, or anything else, you will stay trapped in an unhealthy space.

RATHER THAN ASKING YOURSELF 'WHO, OR WHAT, IS TO *blame*?', ASK YOURSELF, 'WHAT CAN I *learn* FROM THIS? WHAT IS THE *gift* IN THIS FOR ME?'

By refusing to blame anything outside yourself and looking for the hidden gift, you're taking back the power—the power to see the situation for what it really is, take that learning and use it to have a remarkable conversation.

So what gold did I find? Could it be possibly true that I rush through thinking? Yep. Could it possibly be true that I don't always hear from the quiet thinkers unless I ask them? Yep. Could I slow down a little and still have a leadership style that's just as effective, if not better? Yep.

And there lies the gold! You only find it if you bother to go looking for it.

Meditate or do yoga

Neuroscientist Sara Lazar's amazing brain scans show how meditation can actually change the size of key regions of our brain, improving our memory and making us more empathetic, compassionate and resilient under stress. She consolidated the research and data she could find, and it turns out that yoga and meditation practice can result in:

- a reduction of stress
- improvement in anxiety disorders, depression, pain and insomnia
- an increased ability to pay attention
- a better quality of life.

When you do something over and over again in your brain it leads to changes. This is called neuroplasticity. Your brain is flexible; your neurons can change with your experiences.

Build gratitude into your life

What does gratitude really mean? It's about appreciating the good things in your life. It boosts your mood no matter what frame of mind you are in, increasing those positive feelings, and helping you cope better when the tough times hit.

My mother was an incredible teacher in this space for me. Whenever I experienced something that was challenging or emotional Mum would be there to comfort and support me, and when the grief subsided she would ask me what I learned from the situation. What could I appreciate about the circumstance or experience? She would remind me of how blessed we are living in Australia, not having to worry about education and basic needs, and how lucky we were that we had our health and each other.

Even up until the last months of her life, when she was in hospital having chemotherapy, she remained as positive as she could and grateful for what she did have. She would talk of her family, her friends, her humour and her courage. That fuelled her to the very end.

Everyone has times when they feel grateful for something or someone. This generates positive feelings, and happens more easily for some people than others. There are glass-half-full as well as glass-half-empty thinkers. The good news is that your mind can be trained—and one of the benefits is that the bad things in your life don't stick in your mind as easily as the good ones. This doesn't mean you are ignoring or not dealing with situations and people. It means you cope better with them.

There are many ways to increase gratitude. These are what I consider to be the top three.

1 *Start a gratitude journal.* Dr Robert Emmons at the University of California, Davis, conducted a study on people and gratitude journals (which are journals where you record all that you are grateful for, on a daily basis). Those who kept the journal were in better physical health than those who didn't keep one, and were more optimistic, exercised more regularly and described themselves as happier.

2 *Take pictures.* Take photos of those things in your day that make you smile. It could be as obvious as an incredible view, and as simple as a pattern that you like or a window that inspires you.

3 *Get vocal.* Tell people around you what you like about them, what you appreciate, what you love about them. Words are such powerful tools and too often we use them poorly. Be intentional about making them work for good and see how it makes you feel.

Seek advice

We all have blind spots in the way we see ourselves. These are the patterns of thinking, feeling and behaving that can negatively influence our relationships with other people and our ability to get things done. They often show up when we are stressed. If we really want to get a handle on how we view ourselves and the impact it has—to take a hold of the Board of Directors—then it's essential to ask others how they see us.

Throughout our life and career our ego creates these blind spots that limit our vision of ourselves, and therefore our effectiveness. We don't want to see the real truth about ourselves, so we choose spaces of denial or masking.

Brené Brown, a researcher on shame and vulnerability, tells us that we don't like being vulnerable. We don't like feeling exposed to others. While we do want to improve, we actually are not comfortable sitting in the very space that it requires. To be naked and exposed to the truth is too confronting for most.

Have a look at it this way: people are thinking of us a certain way anyway. The only way we can influence this is to understand what they are thinking. Whether they are right or not is not relevant: it is their perception. Without their perspective we will never know the impact we have on others and the way they view us.

Let's change the paradigm and ask for that feedback. Make it easier for others to share how they view us. Make it easier to know ourselves. And yes, we all have different perspectives based on our own iceberg syndrome (see figure 7.1 on p. 101), our own upbringing and values, beliefs and feelings. But wouldn't it be better to know, so we can have the best impact? We just need the courage to listen.

So ask for feedback from your colleagues at the end of projects, after presentations, after meetings. Ask your friends and family for feedback about what you are like when you are stressed; for their view on how you process information; and what you are like when in discussions with them.

I have a business coach and a counsellor, and they are invaluable in terms of what they mirror back to me. Their advice reduces the BODs in my head and clears my perspective. They help me be a better version of myself. Who helps you? Who do you seek advice from, even if that advice can be hard to take?

You wouldn't drive a car with the windscreen blacked out, would you? You'd be a danger to yourself and others on the road. So why walk blindly into working with others without understanding your own Board of Directors?

Get healthy

This should be a no-brainer, but in today's modern world we can favour computers over exercise, fast food over vegetables and can consider wine to be part of the eight-glasses-a-day hydration regime. I'm not going to bang on about this in detail, but it should come as no surprise that a balanced diet, regular exercise and good sleep can improve our brain health and mental function.

Research into the effect of food on mental function indicates that a balanced diet improves learning and memory, and can reduce the incidence of behavioural problems, depression and other mental conditions.

As far as exercise goes, the Department of Exercise Science at the University of Georgia (great name for a university, don't you think) tells us that doing even 20 minutes of exercise per day helps our brain to function more effectively.

When our brain functions well, we can process situations, relationships and data more effectively. This helps us to not only recognise our BODs but to commit to pulling ourselves out of dysfunctional thinking traps. If you want to put the BODs in their place, reduce the unhealthy rumination in your head, and have as healthy and productive relationships and conversations as possible, take care of the basics.

Be careful of comparison

Comparison is the killer of joy. Comparing yourself to others will take you out. It's a deadly game. Living in comparison is like handing your house keys over to a burglar. Why would you do it? You wouldn't! You shouldn't hand over your heart or your self-worth to someone else, either.

Jealousy is not called the 'green-eyed monster' for nothing. Many of you would have heard of research findings that one-third of Facebook users feel worse after visiting the site: someone else has more holidays, a better car, a happier relationship with their partner...It triggers feelings of envy, jealousy and worthlessness. Why? Because we compare. We let others decide if we are enough.

I was one of the facilitators at a student leadership forum in Canberra attended by more than 250 high-potential students from Australia, New Zealand and the Solomon Islands. One of the big lessons that the students took away was how much they let comparison dictate whether they were good enough to be there and contribute. Many spoke at the end about how they got trapped in this space. As the students shared their life stories with each other over the four days they realised what they saw above the surface was very different from what lay underneath. They realised that they were comparing themselves to assumptions they'd made about others, and that comparison was killing them. It was telling them they weren't good enough.

IT'S NOT *easy*, BUT WHY CAN'T THEY BE AWESOME AND YOU BE AWESOME TOO, BUT FOR *different* REASONS?

Why do we need 'you're better than I am', anyway? A beautiful flower stands next to another beautiful flower and they just flourish together. Let's get better at that. Listen to Oscar Wilde: 'Be yourself; everyone else is already taken'.

* * *

You can build your own personal toolkit by applying any or all of the ideas in this chapter. Change and improvement does require action, and sometimes hard work. It all depends how committed we are to becoming better versions of ourselves.

YOUr CHEAT SHEET

- We may have unhealthy BOD thinking patterns, but we have a choice about whether or not we continue to repeat them. We can climb out of unhelpful thinking when we choose to use some tools to help us get there.

- Stay in your lane. Work on yourself first. If you keep seeing only the things that other people need to improve then you will not be able to own what you need to.

- Learn to recognise and replace your thinking. The more often you notice your thinking patterns the greater the chance you have of changing them.

- Smile! Smiling makes others feel great and has a significant impact on our own sense of wellbeing.

- Build a community of positive people. Find a tribe of people that make you feel good about yourself *and* push you to become a better version of yourself, whether it's comfortable or not.

- Seek advice. Get brave and get bold and have the courage to ask those around you about their perceptions and experiences of you. Not only will you find your blind spots, but you will build trust and deeper relationships in the process.

- Get healthy. A balanced diet, regular exercise and good sleep can affect our brain health and mental function, which leads to better mental performance and stamina to deal with the things we need to.

- Be careful of letting comparison steal your joy. Receiving your sense of self and happiness from comparing yourself to those around you is a fast track to unhappiness. Be yourself and own it.

Chapter 10

EMBEDDING 'remarKaBle' in your organisation

Like many of you, I have attended copious training programs. I have also designed and run hundreds. From these experiences, my research and my observations, I have learnt the following.

- Changing habits is uncomfortable and it requires work. Trying something new is not easy and can be counterintuitive. We don't like pushing through awkwardness, even if it will help us improve. We stay trapped in our fears about having the tough conversations.

- People are often not supported to embed the change. Businesses send people to training programs and expect them to transform, grow and develop overnight—without providing ongoing training, reminders or new systems and processes.

- We are unsure of how to integrate the learning into the workplace. While businesses realise that training is not enough in itself, they are unclear about the 'what next'. How do they ensure the learning sticks? They feel like they should know this stuff but they don't.

Then there are the reasons that people are reluctant to share—yet are very real.

- We are waiting for those around us to step up, and then we will. 'When he does, I will', and 'When she stops, I will too' are common catchcries. If everyone's waiting for someone else to do something, inaction becomes the norm.

- We are stuck in old-school habits. In chapter 1 we spoke about the command-and-control style of leadership, which is all about 'you do as I say'. This style continues even after people attend training. Leaders tell their people, and each other, that because they've had training they 'should be good at this now'.

While I believe that some one-off programs can make a difference, they don't tend to most of the time—unless the individual has made the commitment on their own. Resources, money and time can be wasted unless you choose to embed it.

TRAINING DOES NOT *change* US. IT ONLY *educates* US.

Sending your people to training in isolation of any other elements is like throwing seeds on dry soil in the hope they will grow. It's hit-and-miss (and you're more likely to miss).

I starting playing golf many moons ago. When I first started I spent a few weekends at the driving range, pelting out the balls as hard as I could, as far as I could. It was bloody hard to hit them every time with little sense of direction. When I did hit them there was a great deal of satisfaction.

I then decided to get professional lessons. The teacher knew his stuff and made learning fun. I remembering thinking how awkward it was to learn how to hold the club correctly. I was twisted into poses that made me feel I had the flow of C-3PO from Star Wars, but I hit the ball. I returned to the driving range a few weeks later to try and replicate my new learnings. It felt weird. I kept missing the ball and it wasn't enjoyable. I gave up.

I did not push through that awkward feeling to become better at playing.

To be the change we need to move past the 'awkward' of changing bad habits that don't serve us or those around us. We also need organisations to plan and put in place systems and processes to sustain the change.

Figure 10.1 shows the change interventions that are required to maximise your ROI (return on investment). It does not happen overnight—but it does happen.

Figure 10.1: change interventions

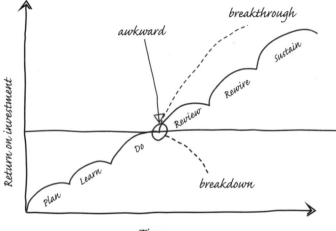

The first few change interventions are relatively straightforward.

- *Plan.* We make sure the design and implementation strategy is right.

- *Learn.* We send people to the training, mentoring, coaching … whichever mode of learning is most suitable.

- *Do.* We go out into the brave new world and put into practice what we have learned. Or we don't.

Here is where the awkward occurs: right before we have a breakthrough. If we don't persevere we can have a breakdown, in which case all that investment in time, resources and money may be wasted. (It often is.) We need to push through the awkward and engage further interventions.

- *Review.* We understand what's working and what's not.
- *Rewire.* We tweak, improve and shift to the next gear.
- *Sustain.* We do not make the mistake of leaving things when they are humming. That's like an Olympic athlete getting a medal and then taking the foot off the pedal. Just because you made it, doesn't mean it will stay that way.

Here's the good news. A breakdown is sometimes what happens just before you have a breakthrough. When you choose to push through. To amplify our investment we need to continue on the 'above the line' breakthrough journey.

Driving change and finding your flow

For your organisation to grow and thrive, it needs to create and foster its own change momentum. I call it finding your feedback flow (see chapter 1). If you want your culture, or your leadership team, to sustain itself after you have run a program to build confidence and develop skills, you need to set up a 'flow', where the learning feeds itself and becomes self-sustaining. Just as a tree needs more than just planting if it is to survive and thrive, so too does an organisation need more than the initial workshop or training. There are many elements involved in making the learning stick.

Peter Cook, a thought leader in implementation, says that people are not wired for long-term projects. We are wired to survive; it's not our natural instinct to think long-term, so we need to put special measures in place to make change stick.

Figure 10.2 shows the five components that contribute to the success of feedback flow in an organisation.

Figure 10.2: requirements for successful feedback flow

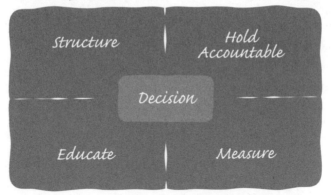

Combined, these components are powerful. It's like baking a cake: you need the right ingredients, put together in the right way, baked at the right temperature. Any of these elements in isolation is a waste. When we set up all five components, the results are sustainable and become habitual.

Make the decision

There's nothing in your way when you're on the other side of making a decision. It's like when you truly decide you want to stick to a new healthy regime: it doesn't matter how many pieces of chocolate cake your partner eats in front of you, because you have decided to be healthy. It's indecision that makes things hard and likely shifts nothing.

I worked with a leader who decided to implement a new database across the whole business. He spent a lot of time sourcing the best program, went through many pitches from potential suppliers, worked with the company accountant to determine the best return on investment and checked in with organisations that were already using the program. He knew his choice was the right one. He was on board.

He designed great training for the users. It was simple, clear and scheduled so that everyone went through it at a similar time. Yet adoption was not smooth—people were not using the new database. Sending out emails to get people on board was not working, the training did not create the shift he required, and neither did telling. We needed to find the root of the problem to work out why things were not changing.

It came down to the decision itself. People had not decided they believed in or needed the new system. They were happy with the old one, as clunky as it was. They did not understand the benefits of the new system and so did not support the change.

When people make the decision to change, or step into something new — whether it's personally or professionally — there are three things that need to happen before the decision can be made.

1 *Believe in it.* Before we adopt something we need to know the *why*. Why are we doing something, what is the benefit, how will it solve our problems, how does it make things better? If we are not clear on the why then we are unlikely to want to move to understanding it in more detail.

2 *Understand it.* Many of us launch straight into doing the work or making the change. We are doers by nature and are often operationally focused. But this is not the first stage; it's the second. We become aware of what the change is, the implications for ourselves and others, how it works, what it does. This is the information phase, where people require detail (some more than others).

3 *Own it.* The next phase is out of other people's control. Only we can now decide if we want to embrace the change. We know the why and the what and how, so it is now up to us to make a decision that changes our mindset from one of gathering information to being on board.

The challenge for organisations is to create an environment that makes the decision as easy as possible.

My client implementing the new database realised that while *he* had gone through the process of believing in it, understanding it and owning it, he had not given his people the chance to do this themselves. He went straight to training, a component of understanding it. But this alone does not create a decision.

Decisions are made all the way through a change process: the decision to ride the wave, the decision to use a new system, the decision to be the change and to be accountable. It underpins all the other components.

Educate with impact

People will only be able to implement and drive what they know or what they are taught. So the quality of the content and calibre of the education methods matter. The better the knowledge transfer the greater the success.

There are four elements to a successful training program:

- set clear and measurable objectives
- design with intent
- create lots of space for practice
- use remarkable facilitators.

These elements form the catalyst to start the change and development of your people and ultimately transform the culture of your organisation.

Set clear and measurable objectives
If you think you can transform an individual or an organisation with a workshop alone then you are kidding yourself. However, the program you use is the foundation of the learning and it needs to be kick-arse to generate the momentum you are looking for.

Agree on the objectives of the program before you design. If you don't know what you want to improve or reduce then it's like playing archery blindfolded—just a game of hit and miss. Some typical objectives that organisations have include:

- eliminating dependence on performance management systems

- improving the performance of staff and leaders

- improving organisational culture through open and transparent communication

- creating a culture of accountability and commitment

- empowering staff to become remarkable givers and receivers of feedback.

Once you know what you want to create, improve and drive, you can design the program to meet these needs.

Design with intent

The design takes into account how your people like to learn, what captures their attention, what impresses and engages them, and the culture of your business. Gone are the days of the cookie-cutter approach to learning. The design also needs to consider educational modes above and beyond classroom-style workshops. It could be coaching clinics, reading materials, online learning, mentoring, immersions or implementation projects.

The design of the program also needs to consider that we all have different learning styles. David Kolb, the founder and chairman of Experienced Based Learning Systems, taught us this in 1984 when he discovered we have individual preferences for the way we retain information. At a simple level, we have a preference for learning in a certain way, whether it be feeling, thinking, watching or doing. When we design an educational program we need to create different ways for people to learn.

Educating your people starts before they step into a training room. It starts with the message the CEO and the leadership team are sending about the program and its objectives, through meetings and everyday conversations. It's about the communications that are going out to excite.

Take it online

There are many forms of education—classroom learning is not the only way. Just look at the Khan Academy founded by Sal Khan, which is changing the way we look at learning. Deliver the learning online as much as you can so people can watch it in their own time, play it over again when they don't understand, and have it available any time they want to refer to it.

Not all training can be delivered without face-to-face contact, but what online learning does is reduce the class time and ensures it focuses on practice and comprehension, making it more engaging and a better use of time. After all, we have never been busier so we need to make learning work for us.

Create lots of space for practice

Practice is a central component of any change process—personal or organisational. We practice something intentionally until it becomes our default. There is no point in training anyone without giving participants the opportunity to put what they have learned into practice. I have worked with so many organisations that tell me they have already completed feedback or conversation training. Yet there were no results. One of the major reasons for this is that there's little to no room for practice.

Deliberate practice makes an expert. We all know that we can't become an expert by observation. If you don't practise, you won't improve. Reading all the books in the world about painting and going to exhibitions all around the world won't make you an expert painter. You need to pick up the brush and give it a go, again and again and again.

LEARNING WITHOUT *practice* IS LIKE WATCHING A HOW-TO-SWIM VIDEO AND THEN *assuming* YOU KNOW HOW.

Having your first tough conversation using the suggested format might feel daunting, yet you will improve with regular practice. Aside from the structure of the conversation you need to consider keeping others safe, owning your reactions, talking in a way that encourages trust and respect, and work on making it feel seamless rather than completely awkward.

Coming from a very direct family, having the courage to have the conversations with others was not as much of a challenge for me as it is for many others. (I'm not saying it was easy, but it was certainly easier than for others I've worked with.) What was challenging for me was that the content I delivered, and the way I delivered it, was not often that helpful. Just because I made it a regular practice to be 'honest' with my friends, family and colleagues, it did not mean the conversations were always successful. I was good at practising and starting the conversations, but the outcomes were less favourable.

It was not until I started facilitating leadership programs that the penny really dropped. When I started developing content and skills in the space of communicating effectively and being *deliberate* in my conversations, things took a noticeable turn for the better. What I learned was that more repetition doesn't lead to better performance in my conversations. My practice needed to be intentional and I had to use the right tools and techniques.

So how is 'deliberate practice' different to just practice? Dr K. Anders Ericsson from Florida State University is an expert in deliberate practice. Ericsson says that it is a highly structured activity engaged with the specific goal of improving performance, and it allows us to become *as good as* those with natural ability. So it is not just about practice, it is the 'how' of practising that matters.

This is good news for those who feel that becoming a remarkable communicator is as feasible as running a small nation while flying around on a magic carpet. The transformation happens in the middle of deliberate practice until it becomes your default.

Malcolm Gladwell in his book *Outliers* talks about the power of 10 000 hours. He says that one of the components of a highly successful individual is practising their craft over and over again, for 10 000 hours.

So the good news is that with deliberate practice we can all become expert communicators. But yes, it takes lots of practice. But here's the other piece of gold: we talk and communicate all day long. It's not like we need to go somewhere else, set some time aside and find people to communicate with, to practise on. We can start now. According to Gladwell's 10 000 hours calculations, if we were talking 24/7 with deliberate practice then it would only take us just over a year to become expert. So yes, we need sleep and we don't talk to people all day, but you can see that it is not as difficult as you think.

To become better at something that we do every day, we just need to get intentional. So maybe you start with the structure of the conversation, or start with keeping others 'safe', or learn to self-manage your fight-or-flight reactions. The point is to start with something and then keep adding.

COMMUNICATION IS LIKE A *muscle*. THE MORE YOU USE IT THE *stronger* IT BECOMES.

Use remarkable facilitators

You get what you pay for, so make sure you hire facilitators and trainers that make the learning easy to understand, are engaging with the audience and know their stuff. Too many times I have seen organisations try to skimp on trainers, or deliver it internally when they are not the experts, and then wonder why people are not changing or taking the training on board.

My best years of high school were Year 11 and Year 12, when I met my accounting teacher, Mr Marshall. He knew his stuff, made learning easy and I felt like I was truly noticed in the classroom. I felt he was teaching it to me, not just going through the motions of covering the curriculum. It became my best subject and I looked forward to it. Teachers and trainers matter. A lot.

Yes, the quality and variety of the education definitely matters. In saying that, the most common belief system that cripples the development of people and leaders is that sending them to a training program is going to transform them. Setting up systems and processes post-training to ensure it's sustainable is the next key to success.

Structure to remember

People and organisations need structures, systems and processes in place to ensure the learning is sustained outside their education. I talk about these structures as 'remembering rhythms'—rhythms that set us up for success.

Every year in Australia, on the 25th of April, we have a public holiday for Anzac Day to commemorate those Australians that we lost in war, from World War I to more recent conflicts. In recent years we have had the biggest Remembrance Day attendances in history. The numbers keep rising, particularly among the younger generation, who often represent their grandparents who died in battle or returned with permanent battle scars. Do you think that awareness and compassion would increase if we did not have this yearly commemoration? Do you think that recognising the lives lost would be at the forefront of our minds if we did not set up this remembering rhythm? I don't think so.

We need reminders; we need acknowledgement in order for something to grow—just like organisations need more than just training to transform their people. Do you really think that one workshop can transform a person or business? I think not.

I was coaching a partner in a professional services firm, as he wanted to improve the leadership skills of some of the people in his team. He was becoming frustrated, as they were not developing as much as he would have liked. In fact, they weren't developing much at all. He told me he had invested time and money in them, sending them to training courses. He allowed them to take time out from the business and allocated the budget for the programs. But still ... nothing. Nothing of significance, anyway. The team members were still coming to him and complaining about their leaders.

I asked him what he had done to ensure the learning sticks. Had he discussed the training with those who attended so they understood how they could apply it, on a daily basis? Was the training provided by a reputable organisation and facilitator? Had he spoken to the leaders about the feedback he'd received? The answer to all these questions was 'No'. Sadly, after working with leaders for more than 20 years I can tell you that this is not an uncommon result.

Without setting up 'remembering rhythms' to help people recall what they have learned and put it into practice, training is often a waste of money. You might see some short-term changes in the first week or two, but it's unlikely they will stick.

Memory researcher Elizabeth Loftus has identified four major reasons why people forget.

1 *Retrieval failure.* Have you ever felt like a piece of information has just vanished from memory? Or maybe you know that it's there, but you just can't seem to find it. The inability to retrieve a memory is one of the most common causes of forgetting.

   So why are we often unable to retrieve information from memory? One possible explanation for retrieval failure is 'decay theory'. According to this theory, a memory trace is created every time a new idea or concept is formed. Decay theory suggests that over time, these memory traces begin to fade and disappear. If information is not retrieved and rehearsed, it will eventually be lost.

2   *Interference.* Interference theory suggests that some memories compete and interfere with other memories. When information is very similar to other information that was previously stored in memory, interference is more likely to occur.

3   *Failure to store.* Sometimes losing information has less to do with forgetting and more to do with the fact that it never made it into long-term memory in the first place. 'Encoding failures' sometimes prevent information from entering long-term memory.

4   *Motivated forgetting.* On some occasions we may actively work to forget memories, especially those related to traumatic or disturbing events or experiences. The two basic forms of motivated forgetting are suppression, a conscious form of forgetting; and repression, an unconscious form of forgetting.

The concept of repressed memories is not universally accepted by psychologists. One of the problems with repressed memories is that it is difficult, if not impossible, to scientifically study whether or not a memory has been repressed. Also note that mental activities such as rehearsal and remembering are important ways of strengthening a memory, and memories of painful or traumatic life events are far less likely to be remembered, discussed or rehearsed.

Memory loss is one of the most common complaints Loftus sees in her clinical practice. Unfortunately, the ageing process can make it more difficult to bring to mind names, places and things.

So the odds are stacked against us remembering. Let's make it easier rather than harder for our people to excel. We need remembering tools to create self-sustaining rhythms. Each organisation will have different tools to suit their style and culture.

Measure consistently

You wouldn't invest all the time, resources and money in a new product and launch it without measuring sales and customer feedback, would you? So why would you invest your people's time and the cost of developing them without assessing the worth? It seems ludicrous to me, but so many organisations don't do this well.

We need to make sure the training and structures and systems we put in place are actually working. Learning in workshops and training is an important step, but it's not the only one — we need to create momentum. We also need to capture the lessons that come from understanding what is working and what needs tweaking or improvement. Without this measurement you are rudderless, and any steps to create more momentum and energy may be lost.

WE *need* TO MEASURE, MEASURE, MEASURE. WHAT YOU CAN'T *measure*, YOU CAN'T *improve*.

When I worked at The Nous Group, a management consulting firm led by Tim Orton, I saw the power of measuring results in action. Two significant leadership and cultural change programs that I learned a great deal from included one for a federal agency and one for a global financial services firm.

Both programs were focused on dramatically improving stakeholder engagement. One was strongly internally focused and the other was focused on their customers. Both recognised the importance of implementing changes for their people and their customers. The federal agency program was the biggest training program conducted in Australia. It involved all agency staff. Nous was engaged to deliver this cultural change initiative. It involved facilitating more than 1300 workshops for over 3500 staff across all business areas in 31 locations around Australia.

The financial services program was on a smaller scale. The aim was to improve the service provided by the whole of the IT department to the organisation as a whole. It involved hundreds of employees, with a strong focus on the leadership team.

There were consistent learnings from both. The key principles I have taken with me and used successfully since are to measure, report back and improve.

Decide what to measure

Agree on what you want to improve, prior to design and delivery. What will look better as a result of the program? What does the organisation want to reduce or eliminate? How will you know it has been successful or not?

If you are clear on the objectives of the program then this is an easy step. If you are not clear on what you want to achieve then you will not be clear on what you need to measure. This should be set out at the design stage of the 'teach' component.

Measurement is different for each organisation. Highly regulated organisations need many assessment tools and checks to be in place. In more fast-paced, innovative businesses the measurement occurs more in the moment and with less bureaucracy. I work with many leading-edge technology businesses that are savvy and fast-paced and committed to innovation. I also work with those on the opposite end of the scale, whose foundations are built on systems, process, checks and balances. Either way, it's essential to put the right assessment tools in place.

These tools are important but are not to be used to fuel analysis paralysis — organisational navel-gazing, where you get focused on providing the reports but not turning them into action. It's like doing a health and wellbeing pulse-check in an organisation, finding out it is low and then doing nothing about it. That's a fast track to disengagement, which can lead to great losses of people and profit. I've seen it too many times. Unfortunately, you may have experienced it as well.

Report back

You have to report back to maintain momentum. People need to see the results of what they do, to understand how their effort, or lack of, has impacted them. We don't do a blood test and not ask for the results. We don't focus on losing weight and not weigh ourselves or notice it in our clothes; we don't do exams and not look at our marks. It's a yardstick. We like to see our progress to become more motivated for the future. We also need to understand what isn't working so we can make changes for the better.

There is a twofold purpose to reporting the results of the program you are putting in place:

1 to learn what's working and what's not

2 to take responsibility for the results.

This should be the easy part, as you have already decided what you want to measure. This is the 'who and when' element: who needs to be aware of the results for process and momentum to occur, and how often you should be reporting back in.

The larger the program, the larger the number of stakeholders. If it is a success then everyone in the organisation should know; it will create movement and drive further change for the better. This can become your catalyst for change across the business. I often work with businesses one department or location at a time so we can prove to the rest of the business what a difference it can make. Then people start talking and get curious about the changes and want to get some of that magic themselves. The training is only one component of the catalyst for change. Reporting on the results helps everyone to ride the wave of change.

Assess and improve

Mamata Banerjee is an Indian politician who is the first woman to have held the office of Chief Minister of West Bengal. In 2012 *Time* magazine named her one of the '100 Most Influential People in the World'. In September 2012 Bloomberg named her one of the '50 Most Influential People in the World of Finance'. Banerjee is known for her wisdom and honesty. She says:

> Change is a continuous process. You cannot assess it with the static yardstick of a limited timeframe. When a seed is sown into the ground, you cannot see the plant immediately. You have to be patient. With time it grows into a large tree. And then the flowers bloom and only then can the fruits be plucked.

Change and improvement take time. It takes time for people to learn the skills to communicate and collaborate. In saying that, the short-term changes are obvious when colleagues, clients and stakeholders actually have honest, constructive conversations for the better.

Tom Peters is a writer who focuses on business management practices. Tom has found that 'excellent firms don't believe in excellence — only in constant improvement and constant change'. Anything that you implement usually needs tweaking and improvement to really thrive.

You have put tools in place to assess, and you have reported back on the results. The question now is what's working and what isn't — and what do you do with that information?

What is working that we can amplify and do more of?

No point reinventing the wheel if the results are good. The key is to make more of it. People love one-on-one mentoring and feel they get great value from it. Do we hire more mentors in the short term just to embed the learning? Do we record some mentoring sessions so people can see others online? Do we ask if people want to become mentors and then train them to do more?

There is a model for analysis called 'Appreciative Inquiry' (AI). It was developed at Case Western Reserve University, starting with an article written by David Cooperrider and Suresh Srivastva in 1987. Cooperrider and Srivastva felt that the overuse of problem-solving as a model often held back analysis and understanding, because it focuses on problems and limits discussion of new organisational models. And so AI was born, and it is now used by many consulting firms and businesses around the world.

The premise is that focusing on what an individual or organisation is good at makes it easier to replicate and grow than focusing on gaps, which take longer to improve. It is still essential to identify and understand the gaps or weaknesses, but amplifying an individual or organisation's strengths gets results much more quickly.

What is not working that we could change, put somewhere else, do more of, or eliminate altogether?

If survey results after a workshop tell us that the participants like the content but the delivery is average, we could change the facilitators or see if the content needs rearranging. We might have found out that only 50 per cent of the participants are attending coaching clinics after the workshop—and so aren't embedding the learning and workshopping the feedback they need to give or that they gave poorly. Do we need to train the managers in each business unit to do these in team meetings? Do the facilitators need to do these in team meetings instead? Do we need to make the sessions available online so it is easier for people to attend? Do we talk to the leaders about selling the importance of driving change? Do we stop the sessions altogether?

Again, if something is not working it may take longer to improve, but it could just require simple changes for the momentum to return.

Accountability with rigour

In chapter 3 we explored the reasons why we avoid giving feedback or handle it poorly. We also looked at some of the costs to individuals and the business. We know that it's not helpful to avoid the tough conversations. One of the biggest reasons for giving feedback or having tough conversations is that it's very important to hold people to account.

According to the Australian Workplace Relationships Survey, Australian workers are fostering an 'avoidance culture', with

46 per cent of people surveyed saying they would rather look for a new job than contend with a workplace issue, while 48 per cent resort to taking days off when they're faced with a tough time at work.

The national survey, conducted in partnership with the Centre for Corporate Health, one of Australia's workplace mental health service providers, also revealed that the ineffectiveness of Australian workplaces in dealing with difficult problems is having a detrimental effect on employee mental health and wellbeing.

So avoidance is costing us great people and it is holding us back from fostering great cultures. If we don't learn to hold each other accountable through feedback and tough conversations we are putting a corporate noose around ourselves and the organisation.

What happens when a child is being told off by a parent, over and over again, but there are no repercussions? The child continues the behaviour because they are getting away with it. They then become 'challenging' to be around and sometimes people avoid them. The same happens in the workplace. This is no way to drive productivity and success.

When no-one owns the responsibility, things don't move forward. Accountability breeds responsibility. We need to learn to hold others (and ourselves) to account. Clinical psychologist and leadership expert Henry Cloud had it right when he said, 'if you are building a culture where honest conversations are communicated and peer accountability is the norm, then the group will address poor performance and attitudes'. It will happen naturally.

We can see the importance of accountability, but some methods have a greater impact than others. There are four ways to create accountability:

1 you

2 your position

3 your peers

4 your public.

Accountability starts with you

You are your own limitations. It's not your friends, your family, your colleagues, your boss, the company, the government. It's you. Some people do extraordinary things in extreme circumstances. They go against the odds and succeed. Some people have all the opportunities and resources yet do nothing. You need to take personal responsibility for your own success — for becoming a better version of yourself.

Taking responsibility and becoming accountable to yourself is where the next step starts. You can't rely on a system or a process or another person to change you. Being accountable is telling the truth, admitting your weaknesses, saying yes, agreeing to start, relying on yourself to push up the mountain. It's signing on to things that are sometimes tough, it's getting outside our comfort zone, accepting that we can influence.

It doesn't sound like a bunch of excuses (when they start, when they change, when they admit they are wrong, when the conditions are right, when the systems or processes change, when I have time, when they stop doing it).

It starts with integrity. It's putting the supermarket trolley back when no-one's looking; it's cleaning the gym equipment after you've used it, even when no-one is around; it's owning the decision that didn't work; it's putting the toilet roll on the right way when you change it. It's doing the right thing even when no-one notices.

Bottom line, it's about what *you* do to put things into place. No-one can control you, but you. Without committing to yourself that you want to own your stuff, prepare and deliver the feedback, receive feedback well and commit to practising, any other steps are hard work and often fruitless.

Use your position

Your position in any organisation is not just about your title. It's not just about being called a manager, or a leader, or a director or an officer. It is also about how much influence we have with those around us. When I say you need to use your position to hold others to account I mean using your position in the community you work in, plus your influence, to get things done—*through* others and *with* others.

We live in an era when people do not trust or respect people automatically because of a title or tenure in an organisation. No longer are people just happy to be in a job. Nowadays we interview the organisation as much as the organisation interviews us. The command-and-control style or 'do as I say' may work to get the task done in the short term, but not in the long run when it comes to building trust and respect.

You need to be able to inspire and influence, and a title does not do that. Using the 'because I said so' speech is abusing your position, not using it. It's old-school and outdated. I do think a healthy balance is key: both parties need to create the respect they deserve.

In saying that, you need to use what you do have to get things done in a motivating way. So if you can hold others to account because of the position you have as a manager or leader of anything, then do it.

- If you have the ear of the board, use it.
- If you have responsibility that gives you the opportunity to discuss issues with a client, discuss them.
- If your title allows you to hold your peers, your manager or your team and other teams to account, do it.
- If you work with team members that are not committing to their word, tell them.

The point is, if you have any authority in the role you have, or influence through the relationships you build, then use it to hold others to account.

You have to stand up to stand out! If you want to make a change and embed what people have learned, use your position to support the change that is needed.

Make the most of your peers
Many of us are uncomfortable having tough conversations with our 'equals' at work and ensuring we are embedding what we

have learned. But our peer relationships can play a key role in helping us become more accountable.

I recall that years ago a peer of mine had the courage to discuss how I came across to others in the organisation when I ran meetings and presented ideas that I was 'passionate' about. She gave me examples and let me know that I came across as bossy, not interested enough in other people's ideas and that when I cut people off it showed disrespect and impatience. She let me know the impact of my style. It was impressive, I thought. She let me know she was nervous about delivering the feedback but believed I would benefit from the information. She was right.

This made me think how valuable working well with our peers can be. The relationship has real power, and it is just as valuable for growth and development as feedback is from your leaders or your team members.

There are many ways you can work well with your peers to create greater accountabilities and better versions of yourself.

- You can give them feedback when they are doing well. We have learned that positive feedback improves performance even more than constructive. Since this is the easiest to give and it creates the biggest shifts, do more of it.

- You can let them know where they need to be better. Just as my colleague gave me feedback (which was tough to hear but I was grateful to receive), you can give your colleagues feedback. Remember that it is a gift because it is so hard to give. If your peers are not living the values the organisation wants to see, or they need to improve their capability, then let them know.

- You can ask them to hold you to account in areas you want to improve. Give them permission to give you feedback, positive and constructive. Create catch-ups to discuss if you are being the change you want to see. And if not, why not.

Bottom line: have the conversations.

Go public

'Going public' is about letting large groups know what you are planning on doing. It's about holding yourself to account on a mass scale.

When I was a student at Thought Leaders Business School, on the last day of one of our three-day 'immersions' we would take a stand. We would go public on something we were serious about committing to—whether it was a 30-day program for living a healthy life, or completing the book we were writing or pitching a new product to a group of potentials. Whatever it was, we would literally stand and eyeball each other and say we were committed. We were serious. We wanted to be accountable to ourselves *through* everyone around us.

Other examples of going public include using social media to declare your commitment to something, like growing a moustache for Movember, or no alcohol for Dry July, or running a marathon for a cause, or committing to a better work culture. It doesn't mean you will always succeed, but it does mean you are committed and want to be held to account.

This is a scary place because it requires vulnerability. It requires courage to tell others you are going to do something, especially when it's very public. Because what happens if you don't make it? What happens if you don't deliver? Then what? That's why it's courageous and that's why it means you are more likely to commit and become accountable. The more important it is the greater the commitment it requires.

Going public is showing the masses that you mean business. It's the ultimate step. It's about removing the mask and throwing yourself wide open.

So what if you do fail? So what? Learn from it. Share your learnings. There is complete accountability in that alone.

your cheat sheet

Embedding remarkable communication into the culture of an organisation requires work and focus. There are five core elements for 'feedback flow' to become the core of any business.

1 Make the decision. We need to check our people believe in the change. That they understand it—and that they own it and want to drive the change.

2 Educate with impact. Training programs are the start, and a really important one. Set clear objectives and invest in good design.

3 Structure to remember. Make it easier rather than harder for your people to excel. Put in place the structure and systems they need in order to take hold.

4 Measure consistently. What you can't measure you can't improve. It's a no-brainer.

5 Accountability with rigour. What's the point of all the hard work if you don't hold others to account? There are some really clever and effective ways to make use of yourself and your networks to do this.

Chapter 11
DO CHE WORK

This story may be familiar to many of you. I worked with a director who constantly talked about the power of an inspiring leadership team and recounted Peter Drucker telling us that 'culture eats strategy for breakfast'. He would then go and invest very little in his people; and he didn't lead anyone to the values plastered on the walls.

We are in an age where information has never been easier to find. We absorb it at a rapid speed. When I was younger we used to go to the library or the encyclopaedia for information. Nowadays we can google anything on our phone, anywhere, and have hundreds of references. We can quickly gather information that tells us smoking kills, dishonesty ultimately catches up with you, and that relationships break down if we don't invest in them. Yet we do not always act on what we know. People still die from self-inflicted diseases, people still get caught embezzling or making corrupt decisions, and marriages and relationships fail regularly.

It's all well and good to know the right thing to do. But wisdom is combining it with action: working out the right blend of knowledge and implementation. But, as we know, it takes work. You have to fight for wisdom and push resistance out of the way.

KNOWLEDGE IS *accessible*. WISDOM YOU HAVE TO *fight* FOR.

Dr Albert Schweitzer was, according to *Time* magazine in 1949, 'one of the most extraordinary men of modern times'. He was a Nobel Peace Prize winner, a famous missionary doctor who spent his life helping the poor in Africa. One day in Chicago a group of reporters waited patiently for Dr Schweitzer to arrive at the train station. He greeted them but soon after excused himself and purposely walked through the crowd to reach an elderly lady having trouble with her bags. With a gracious smile he picked up her bags and helped her onto the bus. He headed back to the reporters, offered an apology and thanked them for waiting. One of reporters was noted as saying, 'That's the first time I ever saw a sermon walking'.

It's not just about preaching. It's about practising. People learn more from what you do than from what you say. So be the example.

I have been blessed to work with Keith Abraham, who is a renowned author and an expert in leading a life of passion and purpose. He and his work are a living example of practising what you preach. Keith once said, 'I have to become the living example. Not the talking example'. Let's subscribe to this way of thinking and inspire ourselves and others for change.

There's work to be done. Do the work!

As I mentioned in chapter 9, I was one of the facilitators at a student leadership forum in Canberra. The purpose of the forum is to challenge the participants—more than 250 high-potential students from Australia, New Zealand and the Solomon Islands—to be the best version of themselves they can be.

Jock Cameron, the founder of the forum, closed the experience with a speech that truly inspired me and the students in the room. He spoke about intent. Intent without action is just an empty promise. You can't will yourself to win a running race. You are unlikely to have a healthy relationship without deciding to make it work. If you want change you need to combine intent *with* action. It is in this crossover that the magic happens.

Your intent influences your actions, and your actions influence your results. Jock spoke about the power of being a 'culture maker' not a 'culture taker'. Are you someone that observes and silently, or overtly, judges your workplace? Do you think of all the things your organisation could do to be better but not action them? Do you get frustrated at the leadership and not give them the feedback? Are you the culture that you want to work in? Or do you sit back and take what is given to you?

If you sit back and watch negative things happen around you do you then become an enabler? Don't you then become a bystander? I don't think there is anything such as an 'innocent bystander'. Not if there is some action to take and you don't take it—whether it is calling someone out on their behaviour, or trying to fix a wrong, or putting something in place to stop the issue. There is only an 'inactive bystander'.

We need to understand that we have the power to create the very space that we are looking for. It's the spirit of entitlement that is killing people's willingness to get up, get on with it and do the work! Entitlement also encourages the 'us-versus-them' mentality. If you want a different culture, a different strategy, a different relationship, then be a culture maker...not a taker. Have the conversation with the person you need to have it with, action that task, do that thing you have been complaining about. Do the work!

Being a culture maker requires effort, courage, determination, sacrifice and resilience. A culture taker prefers to stay lazy and indifferent, to whinge and complain, to get frustrated and annoyed.

In the *The War of Art* Steven Pressfield creates an accurate and compelling read that explains what resistance is and how it is the enemy. Pressfield tells us that resistance is invisible. It cannot be seen, touched, heard or smelled. It is invisible but its effects are measurable. It's a repelling force. It propels us away from reaching our goals, our potential, our calling.

Resistance plays for keeps. When we fight it, there is little half-time or game over. It keeps going. It comes in many forms.

- I'll do it tomorrow.
- I'll get to it when I feel better.
- I'll action it when I'm closer to my potential.
- I'll deliver it when it's perfect.

Resistance is anything that holds you back from being who you are, doing what you are called to do, being faithful and standing in the space you are called to own. While you might not be able to name it directly, it's getting in the way. So get angry, get annoyed: it's holding you back and it doesn't belong.

Resistance tells *me* that I am not pretty enough, that I can't write the book I started, that I am scarring my children, that I will never have a partner, that I offend people easily. And you know what? Sometimes I feed this and go down a terrible path.

Bodybuilders get stronger when they do resistance training, don't they? Writers only get a book if they keep typing on the computer. Children only learn to read when they keep picking up the book. Programmers only write better code when they choose to keep going, and going, and going. If you give in, you get nothing.

Use resistance to learn from if nothing else. The Dalai Lama tells us that 'the enemy is a very good teacher'. In the case of resistance, he is right.

In what areas of your life do you get taken out by resistance? What is holding you back from dealing with things?

Identify the things that hold you back from becoming a remarkable communicator. Understand what traps you fall into when you act like a dick. Then choose, yes choose, the path you want to take from hereon. We are not looking for perfection.

- Own your stuff.
- Know the tools.
- Practise deliberately.

Then watch your decision-making excel, your relationships grow and your leadership become remarkable.

INDEX

Connect with WILEY ▶▶▶

WILEY
Browse and purchase the full range of Wiley publications on our official website.

www.wiley.com

Check out the Wiley blog for news, articles and information from Wiley and our authors.

www.wileybizaus.com

Join the conversation on Twitter and keep up to date on the latest news and events in business.

@WileyBizAus

Sign up for Wiley newsletters to learn about our latest publications, upcoming events and conferences, and discounts available to our customers.

www.wiley.com/email

Wiley titles are also produced in e-book formats. Available from all good retailers.

Learn more with practical advice from our experts